Cooking Light®

350-CALORIE

recipes • hints • tips

W9-BRJ-011

Oxmoor
House®

Shrimp Saté with Pineapple
Salsa, page 122

Welcome

Cooking Light, America's leading epicurean magazine and authority on healthy cooking, is dedicated to helping its more than 12 million readers eat smart, be fit, and live well.

To this end, the editors are proud to present *Cooking Light Eat Smart Guide: 350-Calorie*. This digest-sized mini-book is filled with 90 fresh, quick and easy, 350-calorie or less recipes, along with hints, tips, and techniques for expediting shopping and food preparation.

With more than 20 years of experience, *Cooking Light* is the authority on healthful cooking. Each recipe has been tested at least twice—often three times or more—to ensure quality and satisfaction. In addition, each recipe meets specific nutritional specifications (350 calories or less) and comes with a complete nutritional analysis to help you to make the best choices for you and your family.

This handy throw-in-your-purse guide offers at-a-glance information to help make shopping and cooking faster, easier, and healthier than ever before. From kitchen secrets that shave minutes off prep and cook times to beautiful color photographs that showcase finished dishes, this quick-reference book is full of terrific tips and techniques to make 350-calorie recipes more nutritious and delicious than ever before.

Dinner never tasted so good and for so few calories!
• Craving a slice of pizza hot from the oven? Try Tomato-Mozzarella Pizza on page 54. It's only **243 calories** and way better than delivery.
• Or maybe a thick restaurant-style juicy steak is your preferred indulgence. Well, dig on in! You can have the Filet Mignon with Sherry-Mushroom Sauce on page 28 for only **219 calories**.

It's our editors' sincere hope that you'll turn to *Cooking Light Eat Smart Guide: 350-Calorie* time and again to make wise food choices for you and your family and that you'll find everything you need to assist you in your quest to eat smart, be fit, and live well.

The *Cooking Light* Editors

ISBN-13: 978-0-8487-3298-1
ISBN-10: 0-8487-3298-7
Library of Congress Control Number:
2009925691
Printed in the United States of America
First printing 2009

Be sure to check with your health-care provider
before making any changes in your diet.

OXMOOR HOUSE, INC.
VP, Publishing Director: Jim Childs
Editorial Director: Susan Payne Dobbs
Brand Manager: Allison Long Lowery
Managing Editor: L. Amanda Owens

Cooking Light Eat Smart Guide:
350-Calorie

Editor: Heather Averett
Senior Designer: Emily Albright Parrish
Director, Test Kitchens: Elizabeth Tyler Austin
Assistant Director, Test Kitchens:
  Julie Christopher
Test Kitchens Professionals:
  Kathleen Royal Phillips,
  Catherine Crowell Steele,
  Ashley T. Strickland
Photography Director: Jim Bathie
Senior Photo Stylist: Kay E. Clarke
Associate Photo Stylist:
  Katherine Eckert Coyne
Production Manager: Theresa Beste-Farley

Contributors
Copy Editor: Rhonda Richards
Interns: Emily Chappell, Georgia Dodge,
  Christine Taylor

To order additional publications, call
1-800-765-6400

For more books to enrich your life, visit
oxmoorhouse.com

To search, savor, and share thousands of
recipes, visit **myrecipes.com**

Cooking Light®

Editor: Scott Mowbray
Executive Editor: Billy R. Sims
Managing Editor: Maelynn Cheung
Deputy Editor: Phillip Rhodes
Senior Food Editor: Ann Taylor Pittman
Projects Editor: Mary Simpson Creel, M.S., R.D.
Associate Food Editors: Timothy Q. Cebula;
Kathy Kitchens Downie, R.D.; Julianna Grimes
Associate Editors: Cindy Hatcher,
  Brandy Rushing
Test Kitchen Director: Vanessa T. Pruett
Assistant Test Kitchen Director: Tiffany Vickers
Senior Food Stylist: Kellie Gerber Kelley
Test Kitchens Professionals:
  Mary Drennen Ankar, SaBrina Bone,
  Deb Wise
Art Director: Maya Metz Logue
Associate Art Directors:
  Fernande Bondarenko, J. Shay McNamee
Senior Designer: Brigette Mayer
Senior Photographer: Randy Mayor
Senior Photo Stylist: Cindy Barr
Photo Stylists: Jan Gautro, Leigh Ann Ross
Copy Chief: Maria Parker Hopkins
Assistant Copy Chief: Susan Roberts
Copy Editor: Johannah Gilman Paiva
Copy Researcher: Michelle Gibson Daniels
Production Manager: Liz Rhoades
Production Editor: Hazel R. Eddins
Cookinglight.com Editor: Kim Cross
Administrative Coordinator: Carol D. Johnson
Editorial Assistant: Jason Horn
Interns: Cassandra Blohowiak, Adam Davis

Contents

350-CALORIE
Stovetop Suppers

Simple Skillet Suppers

Sautéing, stir-frying, and deglazing can be a breeze if you use the right skillet.

THE ONE PIECE OF COOKWARE THAT'S ABSOLUTELY INDISPENSABLE IS THE SKILLET. Most of us use one every day to scramble our morning eggs, make grilled cheese sandwiches for lunch, or sauté some chicken for dinner. Is there one perfect skillet for all those uses? Not exactly—it depends on what you want to achieve.

In the *Cooking Light* Test Kitchens, we reach for a trusty heavy skillet almost as often as the nonstick variety. Here's a quick guide to both types.

Nonstick Skillets

GENERAL USES: quick sautéing and stir-frying meats, seafood, and vegetables

BEST FOR: cooking with very little fat, sautéing delicate foods such as fish, or cooking recipes that have lots of liquid

ABSOLUTELY NECESSARY FOR: scrambled eggs, pancakes, and crepes

LIMITATIONS: don't brown foods or conduct heat as well as stainless steel; shouldn't be placed over high heat; may have plastic handles that can't go in the oven

Heavy Skillets

(such as stainless steel or cast-iron)

GENERAL USES: searing, sautéing, and stir-frying meats, seafood, and vegetables

BEST FOR: browning and creating "crusts" on foods

ABSOLUTELY NECESSARY FOR: deglazing (scraping off browned bits stuck to the pan to use in flavoring the sauce)

LIMITATIONS: can't cook completely fat free (some oil must be added to the pan); delicate foods tend to stick

GUIDE TO *Skillets*

HEAVY-GAUGE BOTTOM: This ensures consistent, uniform heat and reduces scorching and hot spots.

SIZE: We use 10-inch pans most often.

LID: A lid isn't absolutely necessary because you'll use the skillet primarily to sear, sauté, and stir-fry. In a pinch, use a lid from another pan.

HANDLE: It's nice to have one that's heat resistant so your skillet can go in the oven—to finish a meat dish seared on the stovetop, for example. Many manufacturers produce heat-resistant plastic handles, but make sure to check the handle's temperature tolerance before you purchase the skillet.

QUICK&**EASY**

Spaghettini with Oil and Garlic

This classic pasta dish comes together quickly, so it's a good week-night dinner. Just pair it with a green salad and a bottle of wine. Spaghettini is in between the sizes of vermicelli and spaghetti, so either of those is a good substitute. Be careful not to overcook the garlic, as browned garlic tastes bitter. Push the garlic to one side of the pan so it will cook evenly.

6 quarts water	1/2 cup chopped fresh flat-leaf parsley
2 3/4 teaspoons salt, divided	1/2 teaspoon crushed red pepper
1 pound uncooked spaghettini	1 cup (4 ounces) grated Parmigiano-Reggiano cheese
2 tablespoons extra-virgin olive oil	
10 garlic cloves, sliced	

1. Bring 6 quarts water and 2 teaspoons salt to a boil in a large stockpot. Stir in pasta; partially cover, and return to a boil, stirring frequently. Cook 6 minutes or until pasta is almost al dente, stirring occasionally. Drain pasta in a colander over a bowl, reserving 1 cup cooking liquid.

2. While pasta cooks, heat oil in a large nonstick skillet over medium heat. Add garlic; cook 2 minutes or until fragrant or beginning to turn golden, stirring constantly. Remove from heat; stir in remaining 3/4 teaspoon salt, reserved 1 cup cooking water, parsley, and pepper.

3. Add pasta to pan, stirring well to coat. Return pan to medium heat; cook 1 minute or until pasta is al dente, tossing to coat. Place 1 cup pasta mixture in each of 8 bowls; sprinkle each serving with 2 tablespoons cheese. Serve immediately. **YIELD:** 8 servings.

CALORIES 303; FAT 8g (sat 2.9g, mono 3.7g, poly 0.8g); PROTEIN 12.7g; CARB 44.4g; FIBER 1.6g; CHOL 10mg; IRON 2.6mg; SODIUM 603mg; CALC 190mg

347 calories

Vegetarian Pad Thai

We love this meatless version of Thailand's popular noodle dish.

²/₃ cup chili sauce (such as Heinz)
¼ cup packed brown sugar
2 tablespoons water
2 tablespoons fish sauce
1½ teaspoons grated peeled fresh ginger
1 teaspoon chopped seeded serrano chile
½ pound uncooked wide rice stick noodles (bánh pho)
4 teaspoons canola oil, divided
1 (12.3-ounce) package extra-firm tofu, drained and cut into ½-inch cubes
2 large egg whites
1 large egg
3 garlic cloves, minced
2 cups fresh bean sprouts
¾ cup diagonally cut green onions
½ cup minced fresh cilantro, divided
⅓ cup coarsely chopped dry-roasted peanuts
6 lime wedges

1. Combine first 6 ingredients; set aside.
2. Cook noodles in boiling water 5 minutes or until done. Drain and rinse with cold water; drain well. Heat 2 teaspoons oil in a large nonstick skillet over medium heat. Add tofu; cook 7 minutes or until browned, stirring occasionally. Remove from pan.
3. Combine egg whites and egg, stirring well with a whisk.
4. Heat 2 teaspoons oil in pan over medium-high heat. Add garlic, and sauté 10 seconds. Add egg mixture, and cook 30 seconds or until soft-scrambled, stirring constantly. Stir in chili sauce mixture and noodles; cook 2 minutes. Stir in tofu, bean sprouts, onions, and ¼ cup cilantro, and cook 3 minutes or until heated.
5. Sprinkle ¼ cup cilantro and peanuts over noodle mixture. Serve with lime wedges. **YIELD:** 6 servings (serving size: 1⅓ cups noodle mixture, 2 teaspoons cilantro, 1 teaspoon peanuts, and 1 lime wedge).

CALORIES 347; FAT 9.6g (sat 1.6g, mono 3.5g, poly 3.5g); PROTEIN 10.9g; CARB 56.7g; FIBER 2.5g; CHOL 37mg; IRON 2.4mg; SODIUM 935mg; CALC 80mg

CHOICE INGREDIENT: *Rice Noodles*

There are three basic types of rice noodles. The trickiest part of using them is that they frequently come in packages without cooking instructions. But thankfully, a saucepan, boiling water, and few minutes are all you need. The big three:

1. Wide rice stick noodles, also labeled *bánh pho*, have a width similar to fettuccine. Cook 5 minutes in boiling water.

2. Rice vermicelli, also labeled *bún giang tây*. Cook 6 minutes in boiling water.

3. Skinny rice stick noodles, also labeled *py mai fun*. Cook 3 minutes in boiling water.

Store-bought clam juice adds great flavor to a quick pasta dish. Add some crusty bread and a simple green salad to round out your supper.

302
calories

Steamed Clams and Tomatoes with Angel Hair Pasta

1 (9-ounce) package fresh angel hair pasta	⅓ cup dry white wine
1 tablespoon olive oil	1 (8-ounce) bottle clam juice
1 cup chopped tomato	2 dozen littleneck clams, scrubbed
1 tablespoon bottled minced garlic	1 tablespoon butter
¼ teaspoon crushed red pepper	4 teaspoons chopped fresh flat-leaf parsley

1. Cook pasta according to package directions, omitting salt and fat. Drain and keep warm.

2. Heat oil in a large nonstick skillet over medium-high heat. Add tomato, garlic, and pepper to pan; sauté 1 minute. Stir in wine and juice; bring to a boil. Add clams. Cover and cook 7 minutes or until shells open. Discard any unopened shells. Remove clams from pan with a slotted spoon; add butter to pan, stirring until butter melts. Place 1 cup pasta in each of 4 shallow bowls; top each serving with 6 clams, ½ cup broth, and 1 teaspoon parsley.

YIELD: 4 servings.

CALORIES 302; FAT 9.4g (sat 3.2g, mono 3.3g, poly 0.8g); PROTEIN 15.6g; CARB 39g; FIBER 2.2g; CHOL 63mg; IRON 9.5mg; SODIUM 194mg; CALC 54mg

STORAGE TIP: Store clams in an open bowl in the refrigerator, and use them as soon as possible. Do not store clams in a sealed plastic bag or on ice, because they will die.

KITCHEN HOW-TO
Peel and Seed Tomatoes

1

2

Afew tricks make preparing tomatoes for sauces, soups, salsas, casseroles, and gratins an easy task. It may seem as if you're wasting a lot of tomato, but you'll finish with just the parts you need.

1. While you're waiting for a pot of water to boil, cut a 1-inch X into the bottom of your tomatoes. Place tomatoes into the boiling water for 30 seconds to 1 minute.

2. Quickly remove each with a slotted spoon, and drop into a bowl of ice water for 1 minute to stop the cooking process.

3. Remove the tomatoes from the water, and peel back the flaps from the X; the skin will be easy to remove. Slice the tomatoes in half horizontally.

4. With a teaspoon or melon baller, scoop the seeds and pulp away from the flesh, and discard. You'll have two clean sections with about ¼ inch of meat for each tomato. Remove any remaining seeds with your hands.

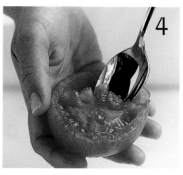

QUICK&EASY

Sautéed Bass with Shiitake Mushroom Sauce

Serve with a spinach-and-mandarin orange salad. Substitute snapper or rainbow trout for the bass, if you wish.

2 teaspoons canola oil
1/8 teaspoon salt
1/8 teaspoon black pepper
4 (6-ounce) skinned bass fillets
2 cups sliced shiitake mushroom caps
1 teaspoon dark sesame oil
2 teaspoons bottled ground fresh ginger (such as Spice World)

1 teaspoon bottled minced garlic
1 cup chopped green onions
1/4 cup water
1/4 cup low-sodium soy sauce
1 tablespoon lemon juice

1. Heat canola oil in a large nonstick skillet over medium-high heat. Sprinkle salt and pepper over fish. Add fish to pan; cook 2¹/₂ minutes on each side or until fish flakes easily when tested with a fork or until desired degree of doneness. Remove fish from pan; cover and keep warm.

2. Add mushrooms and sesame oil to pan; sauté 2 minutes. Add ginger and garlic; sauté 1 minute. Add green onions and remaining ingredients to pan; sauté 2 minutes. Serve with fish. YIELD: 4 servings (serving size: 1 fillet and ¹/₄ cup sauce).

CALORIES 247; FAT 7.6g (sat 1.2g, mono 3.2g, poly 2.4g); PROTEIN 33.2g; CARB 6.9g; FIBER 1.7g; CHOL 140mg; IRON 2.9mg; SODIUM 629mg; CALC 49mg

FLAVOR TIP: Dark sesame oil has a strong flavor and fragrance and is often used for a distinct flavor accent. We often use it in our Test Kitchens in salad dressings as well as for sautéing poultry, fish, shellfish, and vegetables.

247
calories

QUICK&**EASY**

Sweet-and-Sour Shrimp

This Chinese favorite one-dish meal can be on your table in a flash using traditional sweet-and-sour ingredients. Add crunch, not fat, by coating shrimp and tofu with cornstarch, and then pan-fry.

1 (3¹/₂-ounce) bag boil-in-bag rice
8 ounces firm light tofu
2 tablespoons cornstarch, divided
8 ounces peeled large shrimp
¹/₄ cup fat-free, less-sodium chicken broth
¹/₄ cup low-sodium soy sauce
2 tablespoons sugar
3 tablespoons rice vinegar

1 tablespoon chile paste with garlic
2 teaspoons dark sesame oil
2 teaspoons canola oil
1 cup prechopped onion
¹/₂ cup prechopped green bell pepper
1 tablespoon ground fresh ginger
1 (8-ounce) can pineapple chunks in juice, drained

1. Cook rice according to package directions, omitting salt and fat; set aside.

2. Place tofu between paper towels until barely moist; cut into ¹/₂-inch cubes. Combine tofu, 1 tablespoon cornstarch, and shrimp. Combine remaining 1 tablespoon cornstarch, broth, and next 4 ingredients; set aside.

3. Heat sesame oil in a large nonstick skillet over medium-high heat. Add shrimp mixture to pan; sauté 3 minutes. Place shrimp mixture in a bowl. Heat canola oil in pan over medium-high heat. Add onion and next 3 ingredients; sauté 2 minutes. Add shrimp mixture; cook 1 minute. Add broth mixture to pan; cook 1 minute. Serve over rice. **YIELD:** 4 servings (serving size: 1 cup shrimp and ¹/₂ cup rice).

CALORIES 318; FAT 6.8g (sat 1g, mono 2.7g, poly 1.3g); PROTEIN 19.8g; CARB 45.4g; FIBER 2.7g; CHOL 86mg; IRON 2.7mg; SODIUM 681mg; CALC 89mg

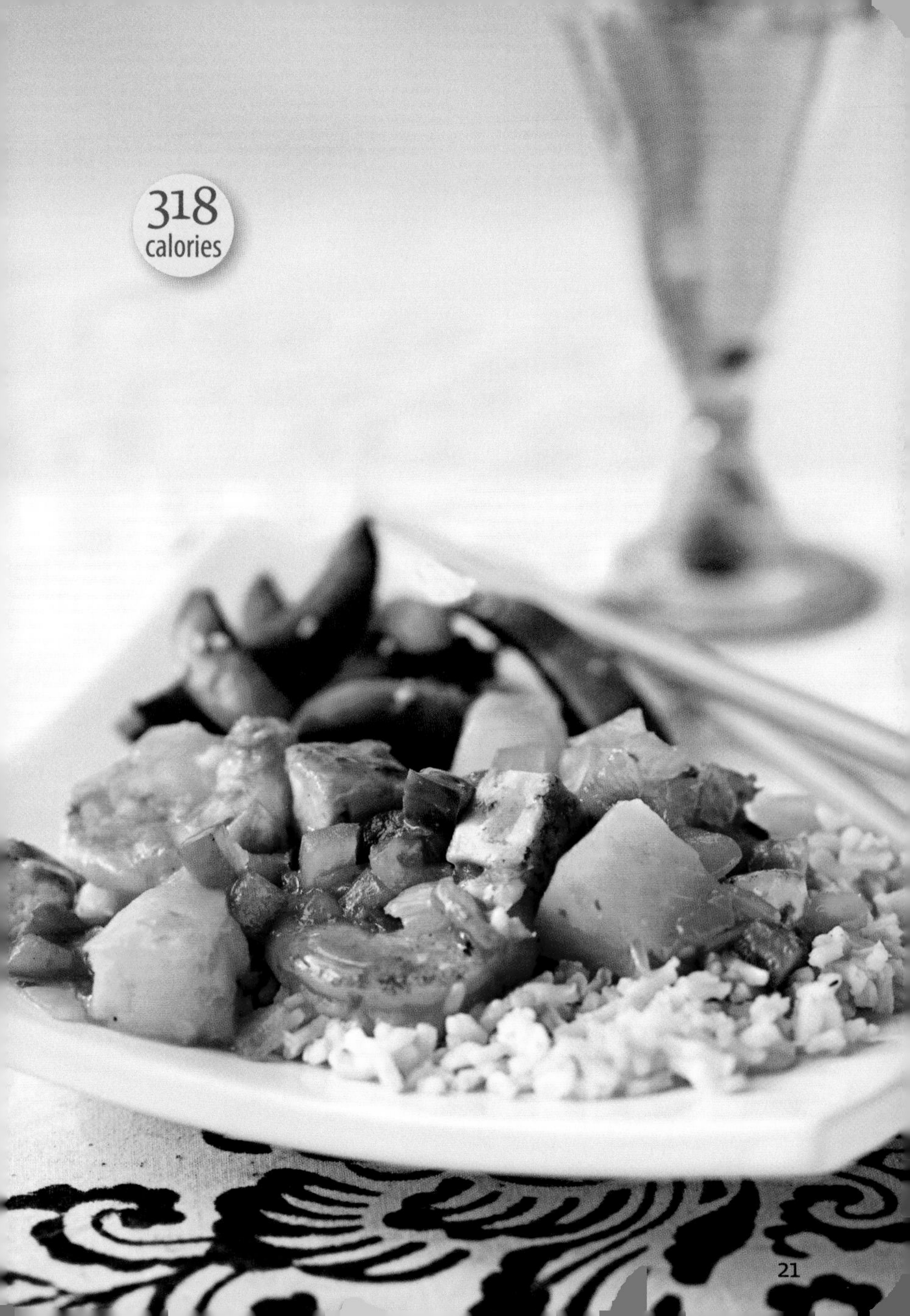
318
calories

Pan-Fried Sole with Cucumber and Tomato Salsa

This simple pan-fried fish is brightened with fresh salsa. Any variety of sole or flounder will work in this recipe. Try lemon sole or butter sole.

- 2 cups quartered cherry tomatoes
- ¾ cup finely chopped cucumber
- ⅓ cup finely chopped yellow bell pepper
- 3 tablespoons chopped fresh basil
- 2 tablespoons capers
- 1½ tablespoons finely chopped shallots
- 1 tablespoon balsamic vinegar
- 2 teaspoons grated lemon rind
- 1 teaspoon salt, divided
- ¼ teaspoon freshly ground black pepper, divided
- 1 tablespoon olive oil
- 4 (6-ounce) sole fillets, skinned

1. Combine first 8 ingredients in a bowl; stir in ½ teaspoon salt and ⅛ teaspoon black pepper.

2. Heat oil in a large nonstick skillet over medium-high heat. Sprinkle fish with ½ teaspoon salt and ⅛ teaspoon black pepper. Add fish to pan; cook 1½ minutes on each side or until fish flakes easily when tested with a fork. Serve with salsa. **YIELD:** 4 servings (serving size: 1 fillet and ½ cup salsa).

CALORIES 175; FAT 5.3g (sat 0.9g, mono 2.8g, poly 0.9g); PROTEIN 25.2g; CARB 6.5g; FIBER 1.6g; CHOL 61mg; IRON 1.1mg; SODIUM 826mg; CALC 40mg

175 calories

QUICK&**EASY**

Broiled Red Snapper with Ginger-Lime Butter

Serve with long-grain rice tossed with green onions. Use any variety of snapper or other firm white fish.

1½ tablespoons butter, softened
1 tablespoon chopped fresh cilantro
1 teaspoon minced seeded jalapeño pepper
½ teaspoon grated lime rind
¼ teaspoon bottled fresh ground ginger (such as Spice World)

¾ teaspoon salt, divided
4 (6-ounce) red snapper or other firm white fish fillets
¼ teaspoon black pepper
Cooking spray
Lime wedges (optional)

1. Combine first 5 ingredients in a bowl. Stir in ¼ teaspoon salt. Cover and chill.

2. Heat a large nonstick skillet over medium-high heat. Sprinkle both sides of fish with ½ teaspoon salt and black pepper. Coat pan with cooking spray. Add fish to pan; cook 3 minutes on each side or until fish flakes easily when tested with fork or until desired degree of doneness. Place 1 fillet on each of 4 plates; top each serving with 1½ teaspoons butter mixture. Serve with lime wedges, if desired. **YIELD:** 4 servings.

CALORIES 202; FAT 6.5g (sat 3.2g, mono 1.5g, poly 0.9g); PROTEIN 33.6g; CARB 0.2g; FIBER 0.1g; CHOL 71mg; IRON 0.3mg; SODIUM 546mg; CALC 53mg

INGREDIENT TIP: One medium lime will give you 1½ teaspoons of rind and 1½ tablespoons of juice. Be sure to wash limes before zesting. For best results, use a citrus zester or a cheese grater (fine grate). Grate only the colored part of the peel; the white part is bitter.

This simple recipe is perfect for hurried weeknights. Sweet, tangy, and spicy, the herbed butter also goes well with shrimp, lobster, sautéed chicken, or beef.

202 calories

The zesty heat of Cajun spices combined with fresh, tropical fruit creates the perfect Mediterranean flavor.

228 calories

Spicy Tilapia with Pineapple-Pepper Relish

Fresh pineapple chunks, now widely available in supermarkets, speed the prep for this relish. Round out menu with a romaine lettuce salad tossed with lime dressing.

- 2 teaspoons canola oil
- 1 teaspoon Cajun seasoning
- ¼ teaspoon kosher salt
- ¼ teaspoon ground red pepper
- 4 (6-ounce) tilapia fillets
- 1½ cups chopped fresh pineapple chunks
- ⅓ cup chopped onion
- ⅓ cup chopped plum tomato
- 2 tablespoons rice vinegar
- 1 tablespoon chopped fresh cilantro
- 1 small jalapeño pepper, seeded and chopped
- 4 lime wedges

1. Heat oil in a large nonstick skillet over medium-high heat. Combine Cajun seasoning, salt, and red pepper in a small bowl. Sprinkle fish evenly with spice mixture. Add fish to pan, and cook 2 minutes on each side or until fish flakes easily when tested with a fork or until desired degree of doneness.

2. Combine pineapple and next 5 ingredients in a large bowl, stirring gently. Serve pineapple mixture with fish. Garnish with lime wedges. **YIELD:** 4 servings (serving size: 1 fillet, about ½ cup relish, and 1 lime wedge).

CALORIES 228; FAT 5.5g (sat 1.2g, mono 2.2g, poly 1.4g); PROTEIN 34.9g; CARB 11.2g; FIBER 1.5g; CHOL 85mg; IRON 1.2mg; SODIUM 328mg; CALC 29mg

QUICK&EASY

Filet Mignon with Sherry-Mushroom Sauce

Place fresh green beans in a bowl with a little water. Microwave 3 minutes or until the beans are done.

4 (4-ounce) beef tenderloin steaks, trimmed (1 inch thick)	1 teaspoon bottled minced garlic
$^1/_2$ teaspoon salt	$^1/_2$ cup fat-free, less-sodium beef broth
$^1/_4$ teaspoon black pepper	$^1/_4$ cup dry sherry
2 teaspoons butter, divided	2 teaspoons cornstarch
$1^1/_2$ cups presliced mushrooms	2 teaspoons water
2 tablespoons chopped shallots	

1. Sprinkle beef with salt and pepper. Melt 1 teaspoon butter in a large nonstick skillet over medium-high heat. Add beef to pan; cook $3^1/_2$ minutes on each side or until desired degree of doneness. Remove beef from pan; keep warm.

2. Melt 1 teaspoon butter in pan. Add mushrooms, shallots, and garlic; sauté 3 minutes. Stir in broth and sherry. Combine cornstarch and 2 teaspoons water in a bowl, stirring until smooth. Add cornstarch mixture to pan; bring to a boil. Cook 1 minute, stirring constantly. Serve sauce over steaks. YIELD: 4 servings (serving size: 1 steak and about $^1/_4$ cup sauce).

CALORIES 219; FAT 10.5g (sat 4.4g, mono 3.8g, poly 0.4g); PROTEIN 25.3g; CARB 3.3g; FIBER 0.4g; CHOL 76mg; IRON 3.3mg; SODIUM 420mg; CALC 12mg

INGREDIENT TIP: Shallots are small onions that have a cross in flavor between an onion and garlic. You can substitute small white onions, although you will miss the unique flavor of the shallot. Use caution when sautéing shallots; they have less water than onions and can toughen and burn easily.

Drizzle frozen mashed potatoes with a bit of truffle oil for a quick but impressive side to accompany this easy dish.

219
calories

QUICK&**EASY**

Pepper and Garlic–Crusted Tenderloin Steaks with Port Sauce

Serve with long-grain and wild rice pilaf and steamed green beans. Although these steaks are simple enough for family weeknight meals, they're good for company as well.

2 teaspoons black peppercorns	Cooking spray
½ teaspoon salt	¼ cup port wine
3 garlic cloves, minced	¼ cup canned beef broth
4 (4-ounce) beef tenderloin steaks, trimmed (1 inch thick)	1 tablespoon chopped fresh thyme

1. Place peppercorns in a small zip-top plastic bag; seal. Crush them using a meat mallet or small heavy skillet. Combine peppercorns, salt, and garlic in a bowl; rub evenly over steaks.

2. Heat a large nonstick skillet over medium-high heat. Coat pan with cooking spray. Add steaks to pan. Reduce heat; cook 4 minutes on each side or until desired degree of doneness. Remove steaks from pan. Cover and keep warm.

3. Add port and broth to pan, stirring to loosen browned bits. Cook until reduced to ¼ cup (about 3 minutes). Place 1 steak on each of 4 plates; drizzle each serving with 1 tablespoon sauce. Sprinkle each serving with ³/₄ teaspoon thyme. **YIELD:** 4 servings (serving size: 1 steak and 1 tablespoon sauce).

CALORIES 205; FAT 7.4g (sat 2.7g, mono 3g, poly 0.3g); PROTEIN 25.5g; CARB 6g; FIBER 0.4g; CHOL 76mg; IRON 2.1mg; SODIUM 389mg; CALC 36mg

205
calories

31

take two:

Filet Mignon vs.

The nutritional breakdown for these cuts of meat is virtually identical. They have similar amounts of calories, protein, and fat. Though you might think of filet mignon as an expensive, special-occasion meat, the price—on a per-serving basis—is just a few dollars higher. And that velvety, melt-in-your-mouth taste is well worth a little splurge. Plus, you don't even need

Filet Mignon

Flank Steak

a recipe; all you need is salt, pepper, and just a few minutes per side in a skillet.

Flank steaks, on the other hand, usually require a little extra care—marinating, grilling, and slicing across the grain to get the best out of them. So when you're shopping for a quick dinner, consider filet.

Flank Steak

Flank Steak and Edamame with Wasabi Dressing

Wasabi paste, made from Japanese horseradish, has a distinctive strong, hot flavor.

1   (1-pound) flank steak, trimmed
2   teaspoons plus 2 tablespoons low-sodium soy sauce, divided
1/2   teaspoon salt
1/2   teaspoon black pepper
Cooking spray
2   teaspoons dark sesame oil
1   tablespoon bottled ground fresh ginger (such as Spice World)

2   teaspoons bottled minced garlic
1   (10-ounce) package frozen shelled edamame (green soybeans), thawed
1/4   cup rice vinegar
2   teaspoons wasabi paste

1. Heat a grill pan over medium-high heat. Rub steak with 2 teaspoons soy sauce; sprinkle with salt and pepper. Coat pan with cooking spray. Add steak to pan. Cook 5 minutes on each side or until desired degree of doneness. Remove from pan; let stand 10 minutes. Cut steak diagonally across grain into 1/2-inch-thick slices.

2. Heat oil in a large nonstick skillet over medium heat. Add ginger and garlic; sauté 1 minute, stirring occasionally. Add remaining 2 tablespoons soy sauce and edamame to pan; cook 2 minutes.

3. Combine vinegar and wasabi paste in a bowl, stirring until smooth. Place 1/2 cup edamame mixture on each of 4 plates. Top each serving with 3 ounces steak; drizzle each with 1 tablespoon vinegar mixture. **YIELD:** 4 servings (serving size: 3 ounces steak, 1/2 cup edamame, and 1 tablespoon vinegar mixture).

CALORIES 253; FAT 11.9g (sat 3g, mono 3.7g, poly 3.9g); PROTEIN 27.7g; CARB 5.9g; FIBER 0.1g; CHOL 28mg; IRON 2.8mg; SODIUM 653mg; CALC 64mg

253
calories

163 calories

QUICK&**EASY**

Pork Tenderloin with Olive-Mustard Tapenade

A little bit of this tapenade adds a lot of flavor. This quick entrée is great served with couscous and a tossed Greek salad topped with feta cheese.

- 1 (1-pound) pork tenderloin, trimmed and cut crosswise into 8 pieces
- ½ teaspoon salt
- ¼ teaspoon black pepper
- ¼ teaspoon ground fennel
- Cooking spray
- ¼ cup chopped pitted kalamata olives

- ¼ cup chopped pitted green olives or onion-stuffed green olives
- 1 tablespoon fresh chopped parsley
- 1 tablespoon Dijon mustard
- 2 teaspoons balsamic vinegar
- ½ teaspoon bottled minced garlic

1. Heat a large nonstick skillet over medium-high heat. Press pork pieces into ½-inch-thick medallions. Combine salt, pepper, and fennel; rub evenly over pork. Lightly coat pork with cooking spray. Add pork to pan; cook 4 minutes on each side or until done.

2. While pork cooks, combine kalamata olives and remaining 5 ingredients. Serve olive mixture over pork. **YIELD:** 4 servings (serving size: 2 pork medallions and 2 tablespoons olive mixture).

CALORIES 163; FAT 6g (sat 1.6g, mono 3.2g, poly 0.7g); PROTEIN 24.3g; CARB 2.2g; FIBER 0.7g; CHOL 74mg; IRON 2.2mg; SODIUM 590mg; CALC 31mg

CHOICE INGREDIENT: *Kalamata Olives*

Kalamata olives are large, purple-black Greek olives that are often slit before packing to allow better absorption of the olive oil and vinegar in which they're packed. They're juicy and plump with a powerful, bright acidity and high salt content. Just a small amount goes a long way.

236 calories

Pork Medallions with Apricot-Orange Sauce

Serve with steamed green beans topped with toasted sliced almonds.

1 tablespoon olive oil, divided
1 (1-pound) pork tenderloin, cut into 8 (1-inch-thick) slices
1/2 teaspoon salt
1/4 teaspoon black pepper
1 cup thinly sliced onion
1/2 cup dried apricots, sliced

1/2 cup fat-free, less-sodium chicken broth
2 tablespoons fresh orange juice
2 teaspoons bottled minced garlic
1/8 teaspoon black pepper
1 tablespoon chopped fresh flat-leaf parsley

1. Heat 2 teaspoons oil in a large nonstick skillet over medium-high heat. Sprinkle pork evenly with salt and 1/4 teaspoon pepper. Add pork to pan; cook 3 minutes on each side or until browned. Remove from pan; keep warm.

2. Heat remaining 1 teaspoon oil in pan. Add onion to pan; sauté 3 minutes or until tender. Stir in apricots and next 4 ingredients; bring to a boil. Cook 2 minutes or until slightly thickened. Remove from heat; stir in parsley. Serve sauce with pork. **YIELD:** 4 servings (serving size: 2 pork slices and 1/4 cup sauce).

CALORIES 236; FAT 7.6g (sat 1.8g, mono 4g, poly 0.7g); PROTEIN 23.8g; CARB 15.8g; FIBER 1.6g; CHOL 63mg; IRON 2.2mg; SODIUM 390mg; CALC 23mg

QUICK TIP: When slicing dried apricots, coat your knife or kitchen shears with cooking spray. This will keep the apricots from sticking and slowing you down.

222 calories

QUICK&EASY

Spiced Chops with Mango-Mint Salsa

Allspice and mango bring Caribbean flair to this dish. The salsa, redolent of mint, also packs a bit of heat thanks to a dusting of crushed red pepper. A Jamaican beer, such as Red Stripe, would complement this meal.

³/₄ **teaspoon chili powder**
¹/₄ **teaspoon salt**
¹/₈ **teaspoon ground allspice**
4 **(4-ounce) boneless center-cut loin pork chops, trimmed**
Cooking spray
1¹/₂ **cups finely chopped peeled mango**

2 **tablespoons chopped fresh mint**
¹/₂ **teaspoon grated lemon rind**
1 **tablespoon fresh lemon juice**
2 **teaspoons sugar**
¹/₄ **teaspoon crushed red pepper**

1. Combine first 3 ingredients in a small bowl; sprinkle evenly over pork.

2. Heat a large nonstick skillet over medium-high heat. Coat pan with cooking spray. Add pork; cook 4 minutes on each side or until done.

3. Combine mango and remaining 5 ingredients in a medium bowl. Serve with pork. **YIELD:** 4 servings (serving size: 1 pork chop and about ¹/₃ cup salsa).

CALORIES 222; FAT 7.1g (sat 2.6g, mono 3.2g, poly 0.5g); PROTEIN 26.1g; CARB 13.2g; FIBER 1.3g; CHOL 70mg; IRON 0.9mg; SODIUM 201mg; CALC 36mg

FLAVOR TIP: To tweak the taste of the salsa, use lime juice and rind instead of lemon. Or substitute chopped papaya for the mango, if you prefer; look for ripe, golden-yellow papaya that yields slightly to pressure.

Spiced Chops with Mango-Mint Salsa

Roasted sweet potatoes
Cut 2 (8-ounce) peeled sweet potatoes in half lengthwise; cut each
half lengthwise again into 6 wedges. Combine sweet potatoes,
1 tablespoon olive oil, ½ teaspoon salt, ½ teaspoon ground cumin,
and ⅛ teaspoon ground red pepper in a bowl; toss gently to coat.
Place wedges on a baking sheet; bake at 425° for 25 minutes or
until tender.

Sautéed baby spinach

QUICK&EASY

Peanut-Crusted Chicken with Pineapple Salsa

Pick up a container of fresh pineapple chunks in the produce section of the supermarket; chop into 1/2-inch pieces for the salsa. Serve with steamed broccoli and warm rolls to complete this 20-minute dinner.

1 cup chopped fresh pineapple
2 tablespoons chopped fresh cilantro
1 tablespoon finely chopped red onion
1/3 cup unsalted, dry-roasted peanuts
1 (1-ounce) slice white bread
1/2 teaspoon salt
1/8 teaspoon black pepper
4 (4-ounce) chicken cutlets
1 1/2 teaspoons canola oil
Cooking spray
Cilantro sprigs (optional)

1. Combine first 3 ingredients in a small bowl, tossing well.

2. Combine peanuts and bread in a food processor; process until finely chopped. Sprinkle salt and pepper evenly over chicken. Dredge chicken in the breadcrumb mixture.

3. Heat oil in a large nonstick skillet coated with cooking spray over medium-high heat. Add chicken to pan; cook 2 minutes on each side or until done. Serve chicken with pineapple mixture. Garnish with cilantro sprigs, if desired. **YIELD:** 4 servings (serving size: 1 cutlet and 1/4 cup salsa).

CALORIES 219; FAT 7.4g (sat 1.1g, mono 3.4g, poly 2.1g); PROTEIN 28.9g; CARB 9.1g; FIBER 1.3g; CHOL 66mg; IRON 1.2mg; SODIUM 398mg; CALC 27mg

219
calories

43

Spiced Chicken Thighs with Yogurt Sauce

The yogurt sauce's cooling effect balances the heat of the chicken.

1 cup uncooked couscous
1 teaspoon ground cumin
1 teaspoon ground coriander
1 teaspoon ground turmeric
¼ teaspoon ground ginger
¼ teaspoon ground red pepper
½ teaspoon salt, divided
8 skinless, boneless chicken thighs (about 1½ pounds)

Cooking spray
¼ cup chopped fresh cilantro
1 teaspoon bottled minced garlic
1 (6-ounce) carton plain fat-free yogurt
Cilantro sprigs (optional)

1. Cook couscous according to package directions, omitting salt and fat.

2. Combine cumin and next 4 ingredients in a bowl; stir in ¼ teaspoon salt. Sprinkle spice mixture over chicken. Heat a large nonstick skillet over medium heat. Coat pan with cooking spray. Add chicken to pan; cook 6 minutes on each side or until done.

3. Combine ¼ teaspoon salt, chopped cilantro, garlic, and yogurt in a bowl, stirring well. Serve with chicken and couscous. Garnish with cilantro sprigs, if desired. **YIELD:** 4 servings (serving size: 2 chicken thighs, about ¼ cup yogurt mixture, and ½ cup couscous).

CALORIES 335; FAT 11.7g (sat 3.3g, mono 4.4g, poly 2.7g); PROTEIN 32.6g; CARB 22.5g; FIBER 1.5g; CHOL 100mg; IRON 2.2mg; SODIUM 425mg; CALC 111mg

335
calories

The pairing of dried fruit and olives is characteristic of North African cuisines, such as Tunisian and Algerian. Serve over Israeli couscous, and sprinkle with chopped green onions.

346 calories

Moroccan Chicken with Fruit and Olive Topping

1	tablespoon olive oil, divided	³/₄	cup dried mixed fruit
¹/₂	teaspoon salt	¹/₂	cup dry white wine
¹/₄	teaspoon black pepper	¹/₂	cup fat-free, less-sodium
¹/₄	teaspoon dried thyme		chicken broth
4	(6-ounce) skinless, boneless	¹/₄	cup chopped pitted green
	chicken breasts		olives
¹/₂	cup prechopped onion	¹/₈	teaspoon salt
2	teaspoons bottled minced garlic	¹/₈	teaspoon black pepper

1. Heat 2 teaspoons oil in a large nonstick skillet over medium-high heat. Sprinkle ¹/₂ teaspoon salt, ¹/₄ teaspoon pepper, and thyme evenly over chicken. Add chicken to pan; cook 4 minutes on each side or until done. Remove from pan; cover and keep warm.
2. Heat remaining 1 teaspoon oil in pan. Add onion to pan; sauté 2 minutes or until tender. Add garlic to pan; sauté 30 seconds. Add fruit and remaining ingredients to pan; cook 5 minutes or until liquid almost evaporates. **YIELD:** 4 servings (serving size: 1 chicken breast half and about ¹/₃ cup fruit mixture).

CALORIES 346; FAT 7.5g (sat 1g, mono 4.3g, poly 1.3g); PROTEIN 40.6g; CARB 26g; FIBER 2.1g; CHOL 99mg; IRON 2.4mg; SODIUM 591mg; CALC 45mg

STORAGE TIP: If you purchase whole fresh onion rather than prechopped onion, store any remaining onion, chopped, in the freezer in a heavy-duty zip-top bag for handy use at a moment's notice. Whole onions will keep for several months in a cool, dry, dark place.

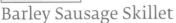

337 calories

Barley Sausage Skillet

Madeira is a slightly sweet Portuguese fortified wine. Substitute sherry or fruity white wine, if necessary. Serve with broccoli sautéed with garlic and lemon.

1 (14-ounce) can fat-free, less-sodium chicken broth	½ cup chopped red bell pepper
1 cup quick-cooking barley	1 (8-ounce) package presliced mushrooms
Cooking spray	2 teaspoons bottled minced garlic
8 ounces hot turkey Italian sausage	2 tablespoons Madeira wine
1 teaspoon olive oil	¼ cup thinly sliced fresh basil
1 cup chopped onion	⅛ teaspoon black pepper

1. Place broth in a small saucepan; bring to a boil. Add barley to pan. Cover, reduce heat, and simmer 10 minutes or until liquid is absorbed.

2. Heat a large nonstick skillet over medium-high heat. Coat pan with cooking spray. Remove casings from sausage. Add sausage to pan; cook 3 minutes, stirring to crumble. Transfer to a bowl. Heat oil in pan over medium-high heat. Add onion, bell pepper, and mushrooms; sauté 4 minutes or until liquid evaporates. Add garlic; sauté 1 minute. Return sausage to pan. Stir in Madeira; sauté 2 minutes. Add barley; cook 1 minute or until thoroughly heated. Remove from heat; stir in basil and black pepper. **YIELD:** 4 servings (serving size: 1¼ cups).

CALORIES 337; FAT 8.1g (sat 3.7g, mono 2.6g, poly 1.6g); PROTEIN 17.6g; CARB 49.1g; FIBER 9.6g; CHOL 34mg; IRON 3mg; SODIUM 537mg; CALC 49mg

CHOICE INGREDIENT: *Barley*

Barley enjoyed its heyday in ancient times when Greek coins were decorated with its fronds, and Roman gladiators (called "barley men") were fed on its porridge. Reasons to honor this nutty, earthy cereal still abound, even if wheat has taken its place as the most common grain in many diets. Barley makes the malt that is used for brewing beer and distilling whiskey (which may be why it was first cultivated). In soups, it releases thickening starches and contributes a soft, chewy texture. And it makes a healthful addition to cereals and breads, providing protein, fiber, and B vitamins. The grains are most commonly found on grocery store shelves in their pearled or quick-cooking variety. Tougher husked types, although richer in nutrients, require overnight soaking.

350-CALORIE RECIPES
Hot from the Oven

Suppertime Shortcuts

When you don't have much time, use some favorite shortcuts from *Cooking Light* to simplify your meal preparations.

1. Keep your pantry, fridge, and freezer well-stocked.

2. Save prep and cook time with convenient potato products, such as refrigerated or frozen wedges, quarters, hash browns, and mashed potatoes. If you're using fresh potatoes, leave the skin on to save prep time and to preserve nutrients and fiber.

3. Forgo coring, peeling, and slicing fresh fruit yourself. Look in the produce section for presliced apple; seeded or unseeded melon chunks; cored pineapple; and bottles of sliced fresh citrus sections, mango, and papaya.

4. Eliminate chopping and slicing veggies by using packaged prechopped vegetables from the produce section, such as broccoli florets, shredded cabbage or angel hair slaw, carrots, celery, mixed stir-fry vegetables, and onion.

5. Gather and prepare all of your ingredients before you start cooking.

6. For quick-cooking chicken, use breast tenders because they cook more quickly than breasts. Or use one of the many precooked chicken products now available: rotisserie chicken, packaged preshredded or grilled chicken, or chopped frozen chicken. Or cook a large amount of chicken to cut and freeze for later use.

7. Buy peeled and deveined shrimp. Ask someone in your seafood department to cook your shrimp while you finish your grocery shopping.

8. Add flavor to meats or side dishes with bottled minced garlic (2 teaspoons bottled equals 4 cloves fresh), or keep bottled whole peeled garlic cloves on hand.

9. Simplify your side dishes by using couscous, quick-cooking grits, boil-in-bag rice, and fresh pasta (it cooks more quickly than prepackaged dry).

10. Use baby spinach instead of regular fresh spinach, and you won't have to trim stems or chop.

Tomato-Mozzarella Pizza

1 (11-ounce) can refrigerated
    French bread dough
2 tablespoons yellow cornmeal
Cooking spray
1½ pounds plum tomatoes, thinly
    sliced
1 garlic clove, minced

1 cup (4 ounces) shredded
    part-skim mozzarella cheese,
    divided
¼ teaspoon black pepper
2 ounces pancetta
¼ cup thinly sliced fresh basil

1. Preheat oven to 450°.

2. Place dough on a baking sheet sprinkled with cornmeal; press dough into a 12-inch circle. Crimp edges of dough with fingers to form a rim. Lightly spray surface of dough with cooking spray. Bake at 450° for 8 minutes. Remove crust from oven.

3. Arrange tomato slices on paper towels. Cover with additional paper towels; let stand 5 minutes. Sprinkle garlic evenly over surface of dough; sprinkle ½ cup cheese evenly over dough. Arrange tomato slices on top of cheese; sprinkle with pepper. Top with ½ cup cheese. Bake at 450° for 5 minutes.

4. Chop pancetta. Cook pancetta in a nonstick skillet over medium heat until crisp; drain. Sprinkle pancetta over pizza; bake an additional 1 minute or until crust is golden. Sprinkle basil over pizza; let stand 2 minutes. Cut into 6 wedges. YIELD: 6 servings (serving size: 1 wedge).

CALORIES 243; FAT 8.6g (sat 4.2g, mono 1.1g, poly 0.2g); PROTEIN 11.5g; CARB 31.7g; FIBER 2.4g; CHOL 17mg; IRON 1.9mg; SODIUM 560mg; CALC 153mg

CHOICE INGREDIENT: Pancetta is an Italian bacon cured with salt, pepper, and other spices. Look in your grocery's deli section for salami-like rolls, ready for slicing or chopping. You can also find it prepackaged in thin slices.

243
calories

QUICK&**EASY**

Creole Cod

The mildness of cod takes well to bold flavorings such as Dijon mustard and Creole seasoning. Lemon juice, added after cooking, brightens the flavor. Serve with steamed fingerling potatoes and warm cabbage slaw.

2 teaspoons olive oil	4 (6-ounce) cod fillets (about
2 teaspoons Dijon mustard	1 inch thick)
½ teaspoon salt	Cooking spray
½ teaspoon Creole seasoning	1 tablespoon fresh lemon juice
blend (such as Spice Island)	Chopped fresh parsley (optional)

1. Preheat oven to 400°.

2. Combine first 4 ingredients; brush evenly over fish.

3. Place fish on a foil-lined baking sheet coated with cooking spray. Bake at 400° for 17 minutes or until fish flakes easily when tested with a fork. Drizzle juice evenly over fish; garnish with parsley, if desired. **YIELD:** 4 servings (serving size: 1 fillet).

CALORIES 148; FAT 3.5g (sat 0.4g, mono 1.9g, poly 0.6g); PROTEIN 27.2g; CARB 0.8g; FIBER 0.1g; CHOL 55mg; IRON 0.5mg; SODIUM 523mg; CALC 16mg

> **FLAVOR TIP:** If you can't find Creole seasoning, make your own: Combine 1 tablespoon paprika with 1 teaspoon each of salt, onion powder, garlic powder, dried oregano, ground red pepper, and black pepper. Store in an airtight container.

A general guideline for baking, broiling, pan-frying, or grilling fish is to cook it 10 minutes per inch of thickness. Some delicate fish may require less time, as do some firm-fleshed fish such as tuna.

Pesto Halibut Kebabs

Serve this dish with Israeli couscous tossed with toasted sliced almonds, dried cranberries, and chopped fresh parsley.

1½ **pounds halibut, cut into 1-inch pieces**
1 **large red bell pepper, cut into 1-inch pieces**
3 **tablespoons prepared basil pesto**
2 **tablespoons white wine vinegar**
½ **teaspoon salt**
Cooking spray
4 **lemon wedges**

1. Preheat broiler.
2. Place fish and bell pepper in a shallow dish. Drizzle pesto and vinegar over fish mixture; toss to coat. Let stand 5 minutes.
3. Thread fish and pepper alternately onto each of 4 (12-inch) skewers; sprinkle evenly with salt. Place skewers on a jelly-roll pan coated with cooking spray. Broil 8 minutes or until desired degree of doneness, turning once. Serve with lemon wedges.

YIELD: 4 servings (serving size: 1 skewer and 1 lemon wedge).

CALORIES 239; FAT 7.9g (sat 1.2g, mono 2.3g, poly 2.9g); PROTEIN 36.3g; CARB 4g; FIBER 1.2g; CHOL 55mg; IRON 1.8mg; SODIUM 514mg; CALC 104mg

CHOICE INGREDIENT: Halibut's universal appeal and mild quality make it a good companion for a host of ingredients. This firm, white fish is widely available fresh and at its best from spring through mid-fall. Halibut is a good source of lean protein, high in B vitamins, magnesium, and omega-3 fatty acids. According to the American Heart Association, each (3-ounce) portion of halibut contains up to 1 gram of omega-3s.

239 calories

Garlic-and-Herb Oven-Fried Halibut

Batter your fillets in crunchy, Japanese-style breadcrumbs called panko—they bake up so crispy, you'll swear these tender halibut fillets are deep-fried. Serve with red potatoes with herbed vinaigrette.

1 cup panko (Japanese bread crumbs)
1 tablespoon chopped fresh basil
1 tablespoon chopped fresh flat-leaf parsley
$^1/_2$ teaspoon onion powder
1 large garlic clove, minced
2 large egg whites, lightly beaten

1 large egg, lightly beaten
2 tablespoons all-purpose flour
6 (6-ounce) halibut fillets
$^3/_4$ teaspoon salt
$^1/_4$ teaspoon black pepper
2 tablespoons olive oil, divided
Cooking spray

1. Preheat oven to 450°.

2. Combine first 5 ingredients in a shallow dish. Combine egg whites and egg in a shallow dish. Place flour in a shallow dish. Sprinkle fish with salt and pepper. Dredge fish in flour. Dip in egg mixture; dredge in panko mixture.

3. Heat 1 tablespoon oil in a large nonstick skillet over medium-high heat. Add 3 fish fillets; cook 2$^1/_2$ minutes on each side or until browned. Place on a broiler pan coated with cooking spray. Repeat procedure with 1 tablespoon oil and remaining fish. Bake at 450° for 6 minutes or until fish flakes easily when tested with a fork or until desired degree of doneness. **YIELD:** 6 servings (serving size: 1 fillet).

CALORIES 293; FAT 9.6g (sat 1.4g, mono 4.9g, poly 1.8g); PROTEIN 39.4g; CARB 9.2g; FIBER 0.5g; CHOL 90mg; IRON 1.8mg; SODIUM 446mg; CALC 89mg

STORAGE TIP: Fresh fish is firm, bright, and has no discoloration. If the fish smells "fishy" or like ammonia, don't buy it. Store in the refrigerator up to 2 days or wrap tightly in airtight wrap, and freeze up to 3 months.

200 calories

Baked Grouper with Chunky Tomato Sauce

$3^1/2$ cups chopped seeded tomato (about 4 medium)
$^1/4$ cup chopped green onions
$^1/4$ cup dry white wine
1 tablespoon chopped fresh basil
1 teaspoon capers
1 teaspoon bottled minced garlic

1 teaspoon fresh lemon juice
$^1/2$ teaspoon salt
$^1/4$ teaspoon crushed red pepper
$^1/4$ teaspoon black pepper
2 teaspoons olive oil
4 (6-ounce) grouper fillets

1. Preheat oven to 425°.

2. Combine first 10 ingredients in a medium bowl.

3. Heat oil in a large heavy skillet over high heat. Place fish, skin sides up, in pan; cook 2 minutes. Turn fish over; top with tomato mixture. Bring to a boil. Place pan in oven; bake at 425° for 8 minutes or until fish flakes easily when tested with a fork. **YIELD:** 4 servings (serving size: 1 grouper fillet and $^1/2$ cup tomato mixture).

CALORIES 200; FAT 5.7g (sat 0.8g, mono 2.7g, poly 1.3g); PROTEIN 28g; CARB 8.6g; FIBER 2.2g; CHOL 41mg; IRON 2mg; SODIUM 400mg; CALC 73mg

263 calories

QUICK&EASY

Baked Salmon with Dill

The delicate blend of fresh dill and lemon lends just enough flavor to add interest to plain baked fish. Serve with grilled asparagus and mashed potatoes with chives to round out your meal.

4 (6-ounce) salmon fillets (about 1 inch thick)
Cooking spray
1½ tablespoons finely chopped fresh dill
½ teaspoon kosher salt
⅛ teaspoon freshly ground black pepper
4 lemon wedges

1. Preheat oven to 350°.

2. Place fish on a baking sheet coated with cooking spray; lightly coat fish with cooking spray. Sprinkle fish with dill, salt, and pepper. Bake at 350° for 10 minutes or until fish flakes easily when tested with a fork or until desired degree of doneness. Serve with lemon wedges.

YIELD: 4 servings (serving size: 1 fillet and 1 lemon wedge).

CALORIES 263; FAT 15.8g (sat 3.2g, mono 5.7g, poly 5.7g); PROTEIN 28.2g; CARB 0.1g; FIBER 0g; CHOL 80mg; IRON 0.5mg; SODIUM 313mg; CALC 20mg

Dover Sole with Lemon Rind and Pine Nuts

If you don't find sole, choose flounder. Thaw frozen fish overnight on the lowest shelf of the refrigerator.

Cooking spray
3 **tablespoons finely minced shallots**
4 **(6-ounce) Dover sole fillets**
¾ **teaspoon salt**
⅛ **teaspoon freshly ground white pepper**

¼ **cup pine nuts, lightly toasted and chopped**
1 **teaspoon finely grated lemon rind**
⅓ **cup dry white wine**
Chopped fresh parsley (optional)
Lemon wedges (optional)

1. Preheat oven to 375°.

2. Lightly coat bottom of a 13 x 9-inch baking dish with cooking spray; sprinkle evenly with shallots. Arrange fish in an even layer over shallots. Sprinkle fish with salt and pepper. Combine pine nuts and rind; sprinkle evenly over fish. Pour wine around fish, being careful not to dislodge topping. Bake at 375° for 15 minutes or until fish flakes easily when tested with a fork or until desired degree of doneness. Garnish with parsley and lemon wedges, if desired. Serve immediately. **YIELD:** 4 servings (serving size: 1 fillet).

CALORIES 219; FAT 7.9g (sat 0.9g, mono 2g, poly 3.5g); PROTEIN 33.5g; CARB 2.8g; FIBER 0.4g; CHOL 82mg; IRON 1.3mg; SODIUM 583mg; CALC 37mg

CHOICE INGREDIENT: Pine nuts are not nuts at all but are seeds borne on the cones of certain pine trees and are harvested

throughout the Mediterranean and across much of Asia. Like other nuts, they are high in the "good" fats. They're also rather expensive. We suggest toasting them in recipes to make the most of their flavor so that a little goes a long way.

350
calories

Shrimp in Green Sauce

This Iberian dish (pictured at right) is similar to shrimp scampi. Serve with bread to soak up the rich sauce.

3½ tablespoons extra-virgin olive oil
6 garlic cloves, peeled
1 cup coarsely chopped green onions
1 cup coarsely chopped fresh flat-leaf parsley
½ teaspoon salt
½ teaspoon freshly ground black pepper
¼ teaspoon crushed red pepper
2¼ pounds large shrimp, peeled and deveined
⅓ cup dry white wine
6 ounces sourdough or French bread, torn into 6 (1-ounce) pieces

1. Preheat oven to 500°.
2. Place olive oil and garlic in a food processor; process until garlic is finely chopped, scraping sides of bowl occasionally. Add green onions and parsley in food processor; pulse until minced. Spoon garlic mixture into a large bowl. Add ½ teaspoon salt, black pepper, red pepper, and shrimp to garlic mixture, and toss well to coat.
3. Spoon shrimp mixture into a shallow roasting pan, and add wine. Bake at 500° for 7 minutes or until shrimp are done, stirring once. Serve with bread. **YIELD:** 6 servings (serving size: about 5 ounces shrimp mixture and 1 ounce bread).

CALORIES 350; FAT 11.8g (sat 1.8g, mono 6.6g, poly 2g); PROTEIN 37.6g; CARB 19.5g; FIBER 2g; CHOL 259mg; IRON 5.6mg; SODIUM 630mg; CALC 131mg

SAFETY TIP: Don't buy cooked fish or shellfish that is displayed next to it's raw counterpart because there is a risk of cross-contamination. Be sure that it is wrapped separately in a leak-proof package.

HOT FROM THE OVEN

Guide to Shellfish

SHRIMP: You can buy shrimp already peeled and deveined at the seafood counter. In most markets, you can buy it steamed, too. Frozen cooked shrimp is available in the frozen food section.

SCALLOPS: These mollusks are removed from their shells at sea, so when you buy them, they're ready to cook. Fresh scallops should be either creamy white, tan, or slightly pink and not dry or dark around the edges.

CRABMEAT: Instead of cooking fresh crabs in the shell, you can buy a container of fresh cooked lump or flaked crabmeat (you'll need to pick out the shells). Or you can buy imitation crabmeat (surimi), which is cooked and ready to use.

297
calories

QUICK&**EASY**

Mustard and Herb-Crusted Trout

Serve with mashed potatoes and broccoli or another green vegetable.

1½ (1-ounce) slices sourdough bread, torn
2 (6-ounce) rainbow trout fillets
Cooking spray

1 tablespoon Dijon mustard
½ teaspoon dried tarragon
¼ teaspoon paprika
2 lemon wedges

1. Preheat oven to 450°.
2. Place bread in a food processor; pulse until crumbly. Place trout, skin side down, on a jelly-roll pan coated with cooking spray. Combine mustard and tarragon; spread over top of fish. Sprinkle fish with breadcrumbs and paprika; lightly coat with cooking spray. Bake at 450° for 10 minutes or until fish flakes easily when tested with a fork. Serve with lemon wedges. **YIELD:** 2 servings (serving size: 1 fillet and 1 lemon wedge).

CALORIES 297; FAT 10.5g (sat 2.8g, mono 3.1g, poly 3.4g); PROTEIN 37.8g; CARB 11g; FIBER 0.9g; CHOL 100mg; IRON 1.4mg; SODIUM 357mg; CALC 145mg

HOT FROM THE OVEN

194 calories

QUICK&**EASY**

Broiled Flank Steak with Warm Tomato Topping

1¼ teaspoons ground cumin, divided
 ¾ teaspoon salt, divided
 ⅛ teaspoon ground red pepper
 1 (1-pound) flank steak, trimmed
Cooking spray
 1 teaspoon olive oil

 1 teaspoon bottled minced garlic
 1 jalapeño pepper, seeded and
    minced (about 1 tablespoon)
 2 cups grape or cherry tomatoes,
    halved
 ¼ cup chopped fresh cilantro

1. Preheat broiler.
2. Combine 1 teaspoon cumin, ½ teaspoon salt, and red pepper;
sprinkle evenly over steak. Place steak on a broiler pan coated with
cooking spray; broil 10 minutes or until desired degree of doneness,
turning once. Cut steak diagonally across grain into thin slices.
3. Heat oil in a large nonstick skillet over medium heat. Add garlic
and jalapeño to pan; cook 1 minute. Add remaining ¼ teaspoon
cumin, remaining ¼ teaspoon salt, and tomatoes to pan; cook
3 minutes or until tomatoes begin to soften. Remove from heat;
stir in cilantro. Serve tomato topping with steak. **YIELD:** 4 servings
(serving size: 3 ounces meat and about ⅓ cup topping).

CALORIES 194; FAT 7.9g (sat 2.5g, mono 3.1g, poly 0.5g); PROTEIN 25.3g; CARB 4.3g; FIBER 1.2g; CHOL 37mg;
IRON 2.4mg; SODIUM 514mg; CALC 38mg

TASTY ADDITIONS

Soy, Ketchup, and Sesame Marinade

Combine all ingredients in a large zip-top plastic bag; add 1-pound flank steak trimmed of excess fat. Seal bag, and refrigerate for 4 hours or overnight. When ready to cook, remove steak from bag, and discard marinade. Grill steak 6 minutes on each side or until desired degree of doneness. Remove from grill, and cut diagonally across grain into ¼- to ½-inch-thick slices. **SERVES 4.**

¾ **cup low-sodium soy sauce**   ¼ **cup ketchup**

¼ **cup chopped scallions**   1½ **tablespoons sesame oil**

QUICK&EASY

Cumin-Coriander Sirloin Steak

The combination of cumin, coriander, and ground red pepper create a tasty rub for the beef. Brown sugar aids caramelization. Cooking the steak in a preheated cast-iron skillet seasons the steak without having to first brown it on the stovetop.

Cooking spray
1 tablespoon brown sugar
½ teaspoon salt
½ teaspoon ground cumin

½ teaspoon ground coriander seeds
¼ teaspoon ground red pepper
1 pound boneless sirloin steak
(about 1¼ inches thick), trimmed

1. Preheat oven to 450°.

2. Coat an 8-inch cast-iron skillet with cooking spray. Place pan in a 450° oven 5 minutes.

3. Combine brown sugar and next 4 ingredients; rub over both sides of steak. Place steak in preheated pan.

4. Bake at 450° for 7 minutes on each side or until desired degree of doneness. Let stand 5 minutes. Cut steak diagonally across grain into thin slices. **YIELD:** 4 servings (serving size: 3 ounces).

CALORIES 198; FAT 8.6g (sat 3.4g, mono 3.6g, poly 0.3g); PROTEIN 25.1g; CARB 3.7g; FIBER 0.3g; CHOL 76mg; IRON 2.9mg; SODIUM 350mg; CALC 17mg

CHOICE INGREDIENT: Coriander, the dried, round fruit of the cilantro herb, about the size of a black peppercorn, is most often used in it's ground form. It has a fruity aroma.

HOT FROM THE OVEN

MENU • *serves 4*

Cumin-Coriander Sirloin Steak

Sweet potato spears
Peel 1½ pounds sweet potatoes; cut lengthwise into ½-inch wedges. Combine potato wedges, 1 tablespoon olive oil, ½ teaspoon salt, ¼ teaspoon dried thyme, ¼ teaspoon black pepper, and ⅛ teaspoon ground nutmeg. Arrange in a single layer on a baking sheet coated with cooking spray; place in oven on bottom rack. Bake at 450° for 25 minutes or until tender, turning once.

Collard greens

Serve with garlic mashed potatoes and steamed broccoli florets. If you have bottled roasted red bell peppers in your refrigerator, you can substitute them for the pimiento.

QUICK&**EASY**

Lamb Chops with Herb Vinaigrette

$^1/_2$ **teaspoon salt, divided**
$^1/_2$ **teaspoon black pepper**
8 **(4-ounce) lamb loin chops**
2 **tablespoons finely chopped shallots**
$1^1/_2$ **tablespoons water**
1 **tablespoon red wine vinegar**
$1^1/_2$ **teaspoons lemon juice**
$1^1/_2$ **teaspoons extra-virgin olive oil**

1 **teaspoon Dijon mustard**
$1^1/_2$ **tablespoons finely chopped fresh flat-leaf parsley**
$1^1/_2$ **tablespoons finely chopped fresh tarragon**
1 **tablespoon finely chopped fresh mint**
1 **tablespoon finely chopped pimiento**

1. Preheat broiler.
2. Sprinkle $^1/_4$ teaspoon salt and pepper over lamb. Place lamb on the rack of a broiler pan or roasting pan; place rack in pan. Broil 5 minutes on each side or until desired degree of doneness.
3. Combine shallots, $1^1/_2$ tablespoons water, and red wine vinegar in a small microwave-safe bowl; microwave at HIGH 30 seconds. Stir in remaining $^1/_4$ teaspoon salt, lemon juice, olive oil, and mustard, stirring with a whisk. Add parsley and remaining ingredients, stirring well. Serve vinaigrette over lamb. **YIELD:** 4 servings (serving size: 2 chops and 1 tablespoon vinaigrette).

CALORIES 349; FAT 15.2g (sat 5.1g, mono 6.7g, poly 1.4g); PROTEIN 47.7g; CARB 1.9g; FIBER 0.2g; CHOL 150mg; IRON 4.6mg; SODIUM 482mg; CALC 37mg

166 calories

QUICK&**EASY**

Rosemary Pork Chops

Choose these fork-tender chops when you need a superfast meal. They're ready to eat in less than 20 minutes.

2 **teaspoons bottled minced garlic**	¼ **teaspoon black pepper**
1½ **teaspoons chopped fresh rosemary**	4 **(4-ounce) boneless center-cut loin pork chops (about ½ inch thick)**
½ **teaspoon salt**	**Cooking spray**

1. Preheat broiler.

2. Combine first 4 ingredients. Rub mixture over both sides of pork chops. Place pork chops on a broiler pan coated with cooking spray; broil 3 minutes on each side or until desired degree of doneness. **YIELD:** 4 servings (serving size: 1 pork chop).

CALORIES 166; FAT 6.1g (sat 2.1g, mono 2.7g, poly 0.7g); PROTEIN 25g; CARB 1.4g; FIBER 0.5g; CHOL 62mg; IRON 1.1mg; SODIUM 342mg; CALC 32mg

CHOICE INGREDIENT: The silver-green, needle-shaped leaves of this mint family member are extremely aromatic, with a scent and flavor similar to lemon and pine. Those mildly acidic notes make rosemary a nice addition to meats—particularly chicken, lamb, pork, and seafood. "It adds spring flavor to winter meals," says Associate Food Editor Kathy Kitchens Downie, R.D. Both fresh and dried rosemary can be purchased in whole-leaf or powdered forms. Store fresh rosemary wrapped in a damp paper towel and placed in a plastic bag in the refrigerator for three to five days. The dried and powdered versions should be stored in an airtight container away from light and heat and replaced every four to six months. Whether fresh or dried, crush or chop rosemary leaves before using them to release the herb's oils so that they can permeate your dish.

All About Lean Pork

Today's low-fat pork is comparable to chicken. The leanest cuts, such as loin chops, loin roast, and tenderloins, have less overall fat, saturated fat, and cholesterol than equal amounts of skinless chicken thighs. Perfect pork will have a faint pink blush. Let it stand for 10 to 15 minutes after cooking to reabsorb juices and to allow the meat to finish cooking. Overcooking lean pork leads to a tough, dry, dish.

PORK TENDERLOIN It's best to add a spice rub, marinade, stuffing, or flavorful sauce to pork tenderloin due to it's mild flavor. Pork tenderloin is small, so it cooks fast and is an ideal quick supper. It is also great grilled whole, butterflied and stuffed, or cut into medallions and cooked in a skillet.

PORK LOIN Loin on the bone stays juicier and more flavorful than bonelss loin, but the bone makes it more difficult to carve. Pork loin is best roasted, and it's easy to butterfly and stuff. Cooking for a long time over indirect heat in a covered gas or charcoal grill is also a great way to cook pork loin. Pork loin is a more forgiving cut; it's slightly higher fat content makes it harder to overcook than the tenderloin.

PORK CHOPS Chops are great cooked by dry heat—whether pan-seared, grilled, broiled, or baked. For these cooking methods, bone-in chops cut from the rib section are best; they stay moister.

PORK SHOULDER Often labled as "pork shoulder butt" (Boston butt), this large, inexpensive chunk of meat is a well-marbled square cut from the upper part of the shoulder. Sometimes the pork shoulder is sliced into steaks, which are sold as blade chops.

BLADE CHOPS These chops may contain some blade bone as well as back-rib bone. They are too tough and gristly to cook as you would other chops and are best cooked by moist heat to tenderize them. They are often butterflied and sold as country-style spareribs.

A quick spritz of cooking spray on the cutlets before they hit the hot oven enhances the crispness and color of the crust. Serve chicken with baked sweet potatoes and broccoli spears.

QUICK&EASY

Peanutty Baked Chicken Cutlets

2 tablespoons honey
2 tablespoons Dijon mustard
⅓ cup peanuts
1 cup panko (Japanese breadcrumbs)

4 (½-inch-thick) chicken breast
  cutlets (about 1 pound)
Cooking spray
¼ cup peach chutney

1. Preheat oven to 500°.

2. Combine honey and mustard in a small bowl; stir well. Place peanuts in a food processor; pulse until finely chopped. Combine peanuts and panko in a shallow bowl.

3. Brush each cutlet with honey mixture; dredge cutlets in panko mixture. Place cutlets on a baking sheet coated with cooking spray; lightly coat cutlets with cooking spray. Bake at 500° for 8 minutes or until done. Serve with chutney. **YIELD:** 4 servings (serving size: 1 cutlet and 1 tablespoon chutney).

CALORIES 282; FAT 7.8g (sat 1.5g, mono 3.3g, poly 2g); PROTEIN 27.2g; CARB 25.6g; FIBER 1.6g; CHOL 63mg; IRON 1.1mg; SODIUM 299mg; CALC 22mg

FLAVOR TIP: Moist, spreadable, and abundant, honey adds more than sweetness to your cooking—it adds a rich, unique  flavor to foods. It's important to choose the best blend. Orange blossom, clover blossom, sage blossom, and buckwheat are some of the more common types. The general rule states the lighter the color, the milder the flavor. We usually use mild-flavored honeys such as alfalfa and clover. If you wish, you can use a stronger variety, such as buckwheat. When measuring honey, lightly coat your measuring cup or spoon with cooking spray first, and all the honey will slide out easily.

207
calories

Salsa Chicken

Personalize this recipe by using your favorite tomato-based salsa. Or try a fruit salsa such as peach, cranberry, or pineapple. Serve with long-grain white rice.

1 **pound skinless, boneless chicken breasts, cut into bite-size pieces**
2 **teaspoons taco seasoning**
Cooking spray
²/₃ **cup bottled salsa**
²/₃ **cup (about 2¹/₂ ounces) shredded reduced-fat Cheddar cheese**

1 **(4-ounce) can whole green chiles, drained and thinly sliced**
¹/₄ **cup fat-free sour cream**
2 **tablespoons sliced ripe olives**

1. Preheat oven to 475°.

2. Combine chicken and seasoning in a medium bowl, tossing to coat. Heat a large nonstick skillet coated with cooking spray over medium-high heat. Add chicken; cook 4 minutes or until browned, stirring occasionally. Arrange chicken in an 8-inch square baking dish coated with cooking spray; top with salsa, cheese, and chiles. Bake at 475° for 8 minutes or until chicken is done and cheese is melted. Top each serving with 1 tablespoon sour cream and 1¹/₂ teaspoons olives. **YIELD:** 4 servings (serving size: ¹/₄ of chicken mixture, 1 tablespoon sour cream, and 1¹/₂ teaspoons olives).

CALORIES 207; FAT 3.5g (sat 1.4g, mono 1.1g, poly 0.5g); PROTEIN 33.4g; CARB 9.5g; FIBER 2.1g; CHOL 71mg; IRON 1.5mg; SODIUM 587mg; CALC 130mg

CHOICE INGREDIENT: *Green Chiles*

Chile peppers come in four forms: fresh, dried, canned, and powdered. The fresh peppers vary in length as well as in degree of heat. While many chiles are indeed hot, there are a variety of methods to tame them so that the chile contributes its unique flavor, not just its bite. One of the best ways to tame a chile pepper's heat is to remove the chile seeds and membranes, which hold most of the heat-inducing capsaicin. Wear rubber gloves, or wash your hands immediately; otherwise, skin that isn't accustomed to the oils in chiles will begin to burn. As a general rule, the larger the chile, the milder the flavor because the smaller peppers porportionally contain more seeds and membranes, and that is where most of the heat is found.

QUICK&**EASY**

Herbed Chicken Parmesan

308 calories

We recommend rice-shaped orzo pasta with this saucy entrée, but you can serve spaghetti or angel hair pasta instead. Add roasted lemon-garlic broccoli, and your meal is complete.

$1/3$ cup ($1^1/2$ ounces) grated fresh Parmesan cheese, divided
$1/4$ cup dry breadcrumbs
1 tablespoon minced fresh parsley
$1/2$ teaspoon dried basil
$1/4$ teaspoon salt, divided
1 large egg white, lightly beaten
1 pound chicken breast tenders

1 tablespoon butter
$1^1/2$ cups bottled fat-free tomato-basil pasta sauce (such as Muir Glen Organic)
2 teaspoons balsamic vinegar
$1/4$ teaspoon black pepper
$1/3$ cup ($1^1/2$ ounces) shredded provolone cheese

1. Preheat broiler.

2. Combine 2 tablespoons Parmesan, breadcrumbs, parsley, basil, and $1/8$ teaspoon salt in a shallow dish. Place egg white in a shallow dish. Dip each chicken tender in egg white; dredge in breadcrumb mixture. Melt butter in a large nonstick skillet over medium-high heat. Add chicken; cook 3 minutes on each side or until done. Set aside.

3. Combine $1/8$ teaspoon salt, pasta sauce, vinegar, and pepper in a microwave-safe bowl. Cover with plastic wrap; vent. Microwave mixture at HIGH 2 minutes or until thoroughly heated. Pour over chicken in pan. Sprinkle evenly with remaining Parmesan and provolone cheese. Wrap handle of pan with foil; broil 2 minutes or until cheese melts. **YIELD:** 4 servings.

CALORIES 308; FAT 10.4g (sat 5.7g, mono 3g, poly 0.6g); PROTEIN 35.9g; CARB 16.2g; FIBER 1.8g; CHOL 88mg; IRON 2.3mg; SODIUM 808mg; CALC 249mg

MENU • *serves 4*

Herbed Chicken Parmesan

Roasted lemon-garlic broccoli
Preheat oven to 425°. Combine 6 cups broccoli florets, 1 teaspoon grated lemon rind, 2 teaspoons olive oil, ¼ teaspoon salt, ⅛ teaspoon black pepper, and 2 thinly sliced garlic cloves on a jelly-roll pan coated with cooking spray. Bake at 425° for 15 minutes or until crisp-tender and lightly browned, stirring occasionally.

Hot cooked orzo

321 calories

QUICK&EASY

Spicy Honey-Brushed Chicken Thighs

- 2 **teaspoons garlic powder**
- 2 **teaspoons chili powder**
- 1 **teaspoon salt**
- 1 **teaspoon ground cumin**
- 1 **teaspoon paprika**
- ¹/₂ **teaspoon ground red pepper**
- 8 **skinless, boneless chicken thighs (about 1¹/₂ pounds)**
- **Cooking spray**
- 6 **tablespoons honey**
- 2 **teaspoons cider vinegar**

1. Preheat broiler.

2. Combine first 6 ingredients in a large bowl. Add chicken to bowl; toss to coat. Place chicken on a broiler pan coated with cooking spray. Broil chicken 5 minutes on each side.

3. Combine honey and vinegar in a small bowl, stirring well. Remove chicken from oven; brush ¹/₄ cup honey mixture on chicken. Broil 1 minute. Remove chicken from oven, and turn over. Brush chicken with remaining honey mixture. Broil 1 minute or until chicken is done. **YIELD:** 4 servings (serving size: 2 chicken thighs).

CALORIES 321; FAT 11g (sat 3g, mono 4.1g, poly 2.5g); PROTEIN 28g; CARB 27.9g; FIBER 0.6g; CHOL 99mg; IRON 2.1mg; SODIUM 676mg; CALC 21mg

INGREDIENT TIP: When it comes to flavor, thighs rule. Thighs have slightly higher fat content than the oh-so-lean breast. But dark meat with the skin removed has less total fat than the same amount of beef sirloin or tenderloin, a pork chop, or a portion of salmon. Thighs are now widely available boneless and skinless, and they are significantly less expensive than chicken breasts.

Skinless, boneless thighs cook quickly and are more flavorful than white meat, so they need fewer ingredients. Serve with a salad and garlic-roasted potato wedges.

316 calories

Turkey Alfredo Pizza

Collard greens and leftover turkey meld beautifully with commercial Alfredo sauce and nutty fontina cheese, resulting in an easy yet inventive meal. Serve with an herbed tomato-mozzarella salad.

1 cup shredded cooked turkey breast
1 cup frozen chopped collard greens or spinach, thawed, drained, and squeezed dry
2 teaspoons lemon juice
½ teaspoon salt
¼ teaspoon black pepper

1 garlic clove, halved
1 (1-pound) Italian cheese-flavored thin pizza crust (such as Boboli)
½ cup light Alfredo sauce (such as Contadina)
¾ cup (3 ounces) shredded fontina cheese
½ teaspoon crushed red pepper

1. Preheat oven to 450°.
2. Combine first 5 ingredients in a bowl; toss well. Rub cut sides of garlic over crust; discard garlic. Spread Alfredo sauce evenly over crust; top with turkey mixture. Sprinkle with cheese and red pepper. Bake at 450° for 12 minutes or until crust is crisp. Cut into 6 wedges. **YIELD:** 6 servings (serving size: 1 wedge).

CALORIES 316; FAT 10.3g (sat 5.2g, mono 3.5g, poly 1.1g); PROTEIN 19.2g; CARB 35.6g; FIBER 0.6g; CHOL 39mg; IRON 2.5mg; SODIUM 837mg; CALC 351mg

FLAVOR TIP: Rubbing the pizza crust with a halved garlic clove imparts lots of flavor with little effort and no chopping.

Turkey Alfredo Pizza

Herbed tomato-mozzarella salad
Combine 3 cups halved grape tomatoes and 1 cup cubed fresh
mozzarella cheese in a large bowl. Combine 2 tablespoons white
balsamic vinegar, 1 teaspoon bottled minced garlic, 1 teaspoon
olive oil, ¼ teaspoon salt, ¼ teaspoon dried basil, and ¼ teaspoon
dried oregano in a small bowl; stir well with a whisk. Pour dressing
over salad; toss well. Serve chilled or at room temperature.

Peach sorbet

350-CALORIE RECIPES
Go Grill

Secrets to Great Grilling

Here are our top 10 secrets for grilling perfection. For more information on grilling meat, see page 95.

1. BE ORGANIZED. Have the food, marinade, sauces, and utensils grillside and ready to go before you start cooking. Make sure that you have enough gas or charcoal before you start.

2. TAKE THE CHILL OFF. Take marinated meats out of the refrigerator, and let them stand at room temperature for 10 to 15 minutes before grilling. That way, you won't end up with a cold center.

3. COAT THE GRATE. Use cooking spray or oil to coat the grate before placing food on it. This seasons the grill, helps clean it, and helps prevent food from sticking. If using oil, quickly run a paper towel that is moist with oil over the grates.

4. GO LIGHT ON THE SUGAR. Cut down on the sugar in homemade sauces, and avoid those bottled sauces that are mostly sugar and salt. Sometimes all you need to flavor grilled food is a little salt and pepper.

5. KNOW WHEN TO BASTE. Many people ruin great food by basting it too early with sugar-based sauces, which results in charring. To prevent burning, add sugar-based sauces toward the end of the cook time. You can

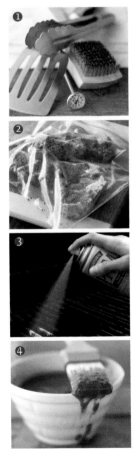

baste with yogurt-, citrus-, or oil-and-vinegar-based sauces throughout cooking. If you use the marinade to baste, stop just before the last 3 minutes of cooking.

6. GIVE IT A REST. Meat will taste better and be juicier if given a chance to rest a few minutes after you take it off the grill.

7. TURN; DON'T STAB. Use tongs or a spatula to turn the meat, but avoid the urge to press on the meat with the spatula. Don't use a carving fork, because it pierces the food and lets out flavorful juices.

8. DON'T OVERCOOK. Know in advance how long you expect to grill the food, and set a timer to alert you to check it. For large cuts of meat and poultry, use an instant-read meat thermometer to gauge doneness.

9. CONTROL FLARE-UPS. Avoid charring meat, and don't eat any part that is especially burned and black. Cooking meats at high temperatures creates chemicals that may increase the risk of cancer. When dripping fat produces a flame in one spot, move food to a different area on the grill. Keep a spray bottle of water by the grill to put out accidental flare-ups. Also, you're less likely to have flames when you keep the oil in the marinade to a minimum.

10. KEEP IT CLEAN. We recommend cleaning your grill twice: once after preheating the grill, and again when you've finished grilling. Use both a metal spatula and a wire brush to scrape the grates clean.

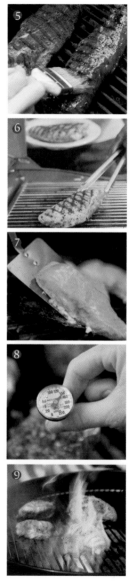

QUICK&**EASY**

Hoisin Grilled Sirloin

Use a grill pan (see below) to make quick work of the steak, or take the opportunity to fire up the grill in nice weather. For colorful and healthful sides, serve with stir-fried snow peas and rice.

2 tablespoons hoisin sauce	**¹/₈ teaspoon crushed red pepper**
1 tablespoon apricot preserves	**¹/₂ teaspoon salt**
1¹/₂ teaspoons fresh lime juice	**1 pound top sirloin**

1. Heat a grill pan over medium-high heat.

2. Combine first 4 ingredients, stirring with a whisk. Sprinkle salt over beef. Add beef to pan; cook 3 minutes on each side or until desired degree of doneness. Let stand 5 minutes before slicing. Brush both sides of beef with hoisin mixture. Cut beef across grain into thin slices. **YIELD:** 4 servings (serving size: about 3 ounces).

CALORIES 213; FAT 8.8g (sat 3.4g, mono 3.7g, poly 0.5g); PROTEIN 25.3g; CARB 7g; FIBER 0.3g; CHOL 76mg; IRON 2.9mg; SODIUM 477mg; CALC 13mg

GRILLING IN ANY SEASON Grilling makes just about any food taste great, but what if it's raining or you're out of charcoal? The solution: a stovetop grill pan. The ridges elevate food so that air can circulate underneath, and fat can drip away. Also the food doesn't sauté or steam as it does in a plain skillet. Meat and fish turn out juicy, with no need for added fat. Vegetables stay crisp-tender, and their nutrients don't leach out into cooking water. When selecting a grill pan, consider the following:

• High ridges: If ridges are too low, you might as well be using a regular skillet.

• Low sides: It makes flipping burgers and removing food with a spatula much easier.

• A square or oblong pan: It fits more food than a round pan.

• A lidless pan: There is no reason to lock in moisture when grilling.

GO GRILL

Nearly half of the grilled recipes in this chapter suggest using a grill pan. Some of our favorites include: Barbecue-Rubbed Pork Chops (page 105); Chicken Breasts with Avocado, Tomato, and Cucumber Salsa (page 109); and Grouper with Puttanesca Sauce (page 114).

QUICK&**EASY**

Steaks with Tuscan-Style Cannellini Salad

Cannellini, large white kidney beans, are common in Tuscan dishes. You can use any white bean, such as great Northern or navy beans.

2 cups chopped plum tomato (about ½ pound)

2 tablespoons balsamic vinegar

1 tablespoon chopped fresh rosemary

1 tablespoon chopped fresh parsley

2 teaspoons bottled minced garlic

1 teaspoon extra-virgin olive oil

1 (16-ounce) can cannellini beans, rinsed and drained

¾ teaspoon salt, divided

¾ teaspoon cracked black pepper, divided

4 (4-ounce) beef tenderloin steaks, trimmed (1 inch thick)

Cooking spray

1. Combine first 7 ingredients in a large bowl, stirring well. Sprinkle ¼ teaspoon salt and ¼ teaspoon pepper over bean mixture; stir to combine.

2. Heat a grill pan over medium-high heat. Sprinkle steaks evenly with ½ teaspoon salt and ½ teaspoon pepper. Coat pan with cooking spray. Add steaks to pan; cook 3 minutes on each side or until desired degree of doneness. Serve with bean mixture. **YIELD:** 4 servings (serving size: 1 steak and ½ cup bean mixture).

CALORIES 291; FAT 11.2g (sat 3.9g, mono 4.8g, poly 0.9g); PROTEIN 27.7g; CARB 18.2g; FIBER 4.6g; CHOL 71mg; IRON 3.4mg; SODIUM 700mg; CALC 59mg

GO GRILL

CHOICE INGREDIENT *Balsamic Vinegar*

When buying balsamic vinegar, look for the words *condimento* or *tradizionale* on the label. Though most of the balsamic vinegars you'll find at the supermarket are just a mixture of grape juice, vinegar, and caramel coloring, Alessi Balsamic Vinegar, which is aged 20 years, is an exception. We also recommend Fini Condimento, a balsamic aged in casks of juniper, chestnut, and mulberry; Gaeta Condimento, aged 4 years in antique barrels; and Cavalli Balsamic Condimento of Reggio Emilia.

Grill Meat Perfectly

While doneness standards can vary somewhat (one person's rare may be another's medium-rare), we follow U.S. Department of Agriculture guidelines for steak temperatures. The USDA doesn't recommend serving rare steak.

Rare [130°] Not Recommended

Medium rare [145°]

Medium [160°]

Medium well [165°]

Well done [170°]

190 calories

Espresso-Grilled Tenderloin Steaks

Try a new twist on the usual weeknight steak dinner. This recipe can be prepared year-round and served with almost any side dish. However, we recommend pairing it with steamed green beans, roasted potato wedges, and red wine.

Cooking spray
1 teaspoon finely ground espresso
1 teaspoon light brown sugar
1 teaspoon steak seasoning
   (such as McCormick Grill Mates
   seasoning blends)

4 (4-ounce) beef tenderloin
   steaks, trimmed (1 inch thick)

1. Heat a grill pan over medium-high heat. Coat pan with cooking spray. Combine espresso, brown sugar, and seasoning in a small bowl; rub mixture evenly over both sides of steaks. Add steaks to pan; cook 4 minutes on each side or until desired degree of doneness. **YIELD:** 4 servings (serving size: 1 steak).

CALORIES 190; FAT 9.5g (sat 3.7g, mono 3.9g, poly 0.4g); PROTEIN 23.5g; CARB 1.1g; FIBER 0g; CHOL 71mg; IRON 1.5mg; SODIUM 245mg; CALC 18mg

GO GRILL

Espresso-Grilled Tenderloin Steaks

Roasted potato wedges
Preheat oven to 450°. Combine 1 (20-ounce) package of refrigerated red potato wedges (such as Simply Potatoes), 2 tablespoons olive oil, ¾ teaspoon salt, ¼ teaspoon ground cumin, and ¼ teaspoon ground red pepper on a jelly-roll pan. Bake at 450° for 20 minutes or until browned, stirring once. Garnish with parsley sprigs, if desired.

Sautéed green beans

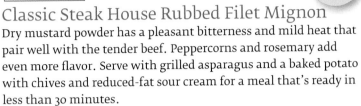

QUICK&**EASY**

Classic Steak House Rubbed Filet Mignon

Dry mustard powder has a pleasant bitterness and mild heat that pair well with the tender beef. Peppercorns and rosemary add even more flavor. Serve with grilled asparagus and a baked potato with chives and reduced-fat sour cream for a meal that's ready in less than 30 minutes.

- 2 teaspoons black peppercorns
- 1/4 teaspoon dried rosemary
- 1 teaspoon dry mustard
- 3/4 teaspoon kosher salt
- 1/2 teaspoon garlic powder
- 4 (4-ounce) beef tenderloin steaks, trimmed (1 inch thick)
- Cooking spray

1. Prepare grill.

2. Place peppercorns and rosemary in a spice or coffee grinder, and pulse until pepper is coarsely ground. Combine pepper mixture, dry mustard, salt, and garlic powder; rub evenly over both sides of steaks. Place steaks on a grill rack coated with cooking spray, and grill 3 minutes on each side or until desired degree of doneness. **YIELD:** 4 servings (serving size: 1 steak).

CALORIES 188; FAT 8.9g (sat 3.2g, mono 3.3g, poly 0.3g); PROTEIN 24.5g; CARB 0.8g; FIBER 0.2g; CHOL 72mg; IRON 3.3mg; SODIUM 407mg; CALC 11mg

QUICK TIP: Look for ready-to-microwave potatoes in your supermarket's produce section. They're prewashed and wrapped in a microwave-safe plastic wrap to speed cooking.

GO GRILL

Classic Steak House Rubbed Filet Mignon

Grilled asparagus with lemon
Combine 1 pound trimmed asparagus spears, 1 teaspoon olive oil,
¼ teaspoon kosher salt, and ¼ teaspoon black pepper in a large
zip-top plastic bag. Seal bag; shake well to coat. Place asparagus on
a grill rack or in a grilling basket coated with cooking spray; grill
3 minutes or until lightly browned, turning frequently. Garnish with
lemon slices, if desired. Serve immediately.

Baked potatoes with chives and reduced-fat sour cream

Open-Faced Burgers with Onion-Mushroom Topping

Use a knife and fork to carve into this tasty burger. Toast an English muffin and then add a seasoned beef patty topped with sautéed onions and mushrooms for a memorable weeknight dinner.

2 teaspoons olive oil
1 medium sweet onion, sliced and separated into rings
2 (8-ounce) packages presliced mushrooms
½ teaspoon salt
2 teaspoons balsamic vinegar
1½ tablespoons paprika

½ teaspoon salt
½ teaspoon dried thyme
¼ teaspoon ground red pepper
¼ teaspoon freshly ground black pepper
1 pound ground round
2 English muffins, split and toasted

1. Prepare grill.

2. Heat oil in a large nonstick skillet over medium-high heat. Add onion, and cook 5 minutes or until golden. Add mushrooms and salt; cook 5 minutes, stirring constantly. Add vinegar; remove mixture from pan. Set aside.

3. Combine paprika and next 4 ingredients. Divide ground round into 4 equal portions, shaping each into a ½-inch-thick patty. Coat patties with spice mixture. Grill patties 4 minutes on each side or until done. Place burgers on muffin halves, and top each burger with ¼ cup onion mixture. **YIELD:** 4 servings (serving size: 1 patty, 1 muffin half, and ¼ cup onion mixture).

CALORIES 320; FAT 10.5g (sat 3g, mono 4.8g, poly 1.2g); PROTEIN 29.4g; CARB 27.3g; FIBER 4.6g; CHOL 70mg; IRON 5.1mg; SODIUM 813mg; CALC 82mg

232
calories

Rosemary Grilled Lamb Chops

Garlic and chopped fresh rosemary lend a heady, fragrant aroma to this lamb chop.

1 tablespoon chopped fresh rosemary	4 (4-ounce) lamb loin chops, trimmed
1 teaspoon olive oil	⅛ teaspoon freshly ground black pepper
½ teaspoon kosher salt, divided	Cooking spray
1 garlic clove, minced	

1. Combine rosemary, oil, ¼ teaspoon salt, and garlic; rub mixture evenly over both sides of lamb. Cover and marinate in refrigerator at least 2 hours or overnight.

2. Prepare grill.

3. Sprinkle both sides of lamb with ¼ teaspoon salt and ⅛ teaspoon pepper. Place lamb on a grill rack coated with cooking spray; grill 3 minutes on each side or until desired degree of doneness (145° for medium rare). **YIELD:** 4 servings (serving size: 1 chop).

CALORIES 232; FAT 15.2g (sat 5.9g, mono 7.2g, poly 0.9g); PROTEIN 22g; CARB 0.5g; FIBER 0.2g; CHOL 72mg; IRON 2.1mg; SODIUM 290mg; CALC 17mg

QUICK TIP: An instant-read thermometer is crucial for determining when to remove the lamb from the grill (from 140° for rare to 170° for well done), as doneness is a matter of personal preference.

GO GRILL

The leanest cuts of lamb are those with the words "loin" or "leg" on the label. It's easy to overcook lean lamb, so watch your cooking time and temperature carefully. If you cook it too long, the meat will be tough.

Barbecue-Rubbed Pork Chops

Cheddar grits
Bring 2 cups fat-free milk and 1¼ cups water to a boil in a medium saucepan over medium-high heat. Slowly add ¾ cup quick-cooking grits, stirring well with a whisk. Cover, reduce heat, and simmer 5 minutes or until thick, stirring occasionally. Remove from heat. Add 1 cup reduced-fat shredded sharp Cheddar cheese, 1 tablespoon butter, ½ teaspoon salt, and ⅛ teaspoon freshly ground black pepper, stirring until cheese melts.

Cucumber-red onion salad

GO GRILL

QUICK&**EASY**

Barbecue-Rubbed Pork Chops

This bold, zesty rub is made up of seven spices. Turn up the heat by using hot paprika or $1/4$ teaspoon ground red pepper. Serve with Cheddar grits and a cucumber-red onion salad.

1 tablespoon light brown sugar	$1/8$ teaspoon ground allspice
1 teaspoon salt	$1/8$ teaspoon ground red pepper
1 teaspoon paprika	**4** (6-ounce) bone-in center-cut
1 teaspoon chili powder	loin pork chops, trimmed
$3/4$ teaspoon garlic powder	(about $1/2$ inch thick)
$3/4$ teaspoon ground cumin	Cooking spray
$1/4$ teaspoon dry mustard	

1. Combine first 9 ingredients; rub over both sides of pork. Heat grill pan over medium-high heat. Coat pan with cooking spray. Add pork; cook 2 minutes on each side. Reduce heat to medium, and cook 8 minutes or until done, turning occasionally. Remove from pan; let stand 5 minutes. **YIELD:** 4 servings (serving size: 1 pork chop).

CALORIES 277; FAT 10.5g (sat 3.8g, mono 4.7g, poly 0.8g); PROTEIN 38.8g; CARB 4.3g; FIBER 0.5g; CHOL 105mg; IRON 1.4mg; SODIUM 669mg; CALC 48mg

Fig and Chile-Glazed Pork Tenderloin

Sweet preserves, tart vinegar, and spicy chile paste combine to create a memorable entrée. Serve this spicy pork with basmati rice and black beans. The glaze also enhances chicken thighs.

1/2 cup fig preserves
1/4 cup rice vinegar
1 tablespoon chile paste with garlic
1 tablespoon low-sodium soy sauce
1/2 teaspoon kosher salt, divided

2 (1-pound) pork tenderloins, trimmed
1/2 teaspoon freshly ground black pepper
Cooking spray
Fresh chives, cut into 1-inch pieces (optional)

1. Prepare grill to medium-high heat.

2. Combine first 4 ingredients and 1/4 teaspoon salt, stirring with a whisk.

3. Sprinkle pork with 1/4 teaspoon salt and 1/2 teaspoon pepper. Place pork on a grill rack coated with cooking spray; grill 18 minutes or until thermometer registers 160° (slightly pink), turning occasionally and basting frequently with fig mixture. Garnish with chives, if desired. **YIELD:** 8 servings (serving size: about 3 ounces).

CALORIES 193; FAT 3.9g (sat 1.3g, mono 1.8g, poly 0.4g); PROTEIN 24g; CARB 14g; FIBER 0.3g; CHOL 74mg; IRON 1.6mg; SODIUM 274mg; CALC 11mg

GO GRILL

We all have jars of sweet jams, preserves, and jellies tucked away in the fridge, waiting for breakfast toast. But there's another use for them: Turn basic and specialty jams and jellies into sauces and glazes for quick entrées.

193
calories

QUICK&EASY

Jamaican-Spiced Chicken Thighs

187 calories

¼ cup minced red onion	½ teaspoon ground allspice
1 tablespoon sugar	½ teaspoon dried thyme
1 tablespoon finely chopped seeded jalapeño pepper	½ teaspoon black pepper
	¼ teaspoon ground red pepper
2 teaspoons cider vinegar	8 skinless, boneless chicken thighs
2 teaspoons low-sodium soy sauce	(about 1½ pounds)
½ teaspoon salt	Cooking spray

1. Combine first 10 ingredients in a large bowl; add chicken, tossing to coat. Heat a grill pan over medium-high heat. Coat pan with cooking spray. Add chicken to pan; cook 4 minutes. Turn chicken over; cook 6 minutes or until done. **YIELD:** 4 servings (serving size: 2 chicken thighs).

CALORIES 187; FAT 5.7g (sat 1.4g, mono 1.7g, poly 1.4g); PROTEIN 27.5g; CARB 5g; FIBER 0.5g; CHOL 115mg; IRON 1.6mg; SODIUM 503mg; CALC 21mg

QUICK&EASY

Chicken Breasts with Avocado, Tomato, and Cucumber Salsa

Cooking spray

¾ teaspoon salt, divided

¼ teaspoon chipotle chile powder

4 (6-ounce) skinless, boneless chicken breast halves

1¼ cups coarsely chopped seeded peeled cucumber (about 1 large)

1 cup grape tomatoes, halved

½ cup prechopped red onion

½ cup chopped peeled avocado

2 tablespoons chopped fresh cilantro

2 tablespoons fresh lime juice

1 jalapeño pepper, seeded and finely chopped

1. Heat a grill pan over medium-high heat. Coat pan with cooking spray. Sprinkle ½ teaspoon salt and ¼ teaspoon chile powder evenly over chicken; add chicken to pan. Cook 6 minutes on each side or until done, and remove from heat.

2. Combine remaining ¼ teaspoon salt, cucumber, and remaining ingredients in a medium bowl, tossing well. Serve with chicken.

YIELD: 4 servings (serving size: 1 chicken breast half and ¾ cup salsa).

CALORIES 243; FAT 7.6g (sat 1.6g, mono 3.5g, poly 1.3g); PROTEIN 35.6g; CARB 7.3g; FIBER 2.7g; CHOL 94mg; IRON 1.7mg; SODIUM 533mg; CALC 34mg

267 calories

Chicken Saté with Ponzu Sauce

This dish calls for a wine that's bold yet refreshing. Dry rosé does this admirably.

4   (6-ounce) skinless, boneless chicken breast halves
¼   cup packed light brown sugar
¼   cup sake (rice wine)
¼   cup rice vinegar
¼   cup fresh lime juice

2   teaspoons low-sodium soy sauce
1   teaspoon dark sesame oil
¼   teaspoon crushed red pepper
1   garlic clove, minced
Cooking spray

GO GRILL

110

1. Prepare grill.

2. Cut each chicken breast half lengthwise into 4 strips. Combine sugar and next 7 ingredients in a small bowl; stir until sugar dissolves. Combine chicken and half of sake mixture in a large bowl. Let stand 10 minutes. Reserve remaining sake mixture.

3. Drain chicken, discarding marinade. Thread 1 chicken strip onto each of 16 (8-inch) skewers. Place chicken on grill rack coated with cooking spray; grill 2 minutes on each side or until done. Serve with remaining sake mixture. **YIELD:** 4 servings (serving size: 4 skewers and about 1½ tablespoons sake mixture).

CALORIES 267; FAT 3.5g (sat 0.7g, mono 0.5g, poly 0.5g); PROTEIN 39.6g; CARB 13.3g; FIBER 0.1g; CHOL 99mg; IRON 1.6mg; SODIUM 216mg; CALC 30mg

GO GRILL

Saté Burgers

Peanuts, cilantro, brown sugar, lime juice, and fish sauce are the typical ingredients used in Indonesian meat skewers called satés. They add flavor to these burgers as well. Using equal amounts of ground turkey and pork keeps these burgers lean. Serve on a bed of brown rice with spinach and lime wedges.

½ cup chopped fresh cilantro
¼ cup finely chopped unsalted dry-roasted peanuts
2 tablespoons fresh lime juice
1½ tablespoons brown sugar
1½ tablespoons fish sauce
1½ teaspoons ground cumin
½ teaspoon salt
¼ teaspoon hot pepper sauce (such as Tabasco)
3 garlic cloves, minced
¾ pound ground pork
¾ pound ground turkey breast
Cooking spray

1. Prepare grill.

2. Combine first 11 ingredients. Divide mixture into 6 equal portions, shaping each into a ½-inch-thick patty.

3. Place patties on a grill rack coated with cooking spray; grill 7 minutes on each side or until a thermometer registers 165°. Remove from grill; let stand 5 minutes. YIELD: 6 servings (serving size: 1 patty).

CALORIES 166; FAT 7.5g (sat 2.1g, mono 3.1g, poly 1.3g); PROTEIN 20.1g; CARB 4.9g; FIBER 0.8g; CHOL 49mg; IRON 0.7mg; SODIUM 599mg; CALC 16mg

QUICK&EASY

Grouper with Puttanesca Sauce

Keep your pantry stocked with the sauce ingredients to make this dish anytime. Serve with orzo to soak up the sauce.

4 (6-ounce) grouper or flounder fillets
¼ teaspoon black pepper
⅛ teaspoon salt
Cooking spray
1½ teaspoons olive oil
1 cup thinly sliced onion
1 tablespoon bottled minced garlic

¼ teaspoon dried oregano
1 (28-ounce) can whole tomatoes, drained
⅓ cup chopped pitted kalamata olives
2 tablespoons capers
¼ cup chopped fresh flat-leaf parsley (optional)

1. Heat a nonstick grill pan over medium-high heat. Sprinkle fish with pepper and salt. Coat pan with cooking spray. Add fish to pan; cook 5 minutes on each side or until fish flakes easily when tested with a fork.

2. While fish cooks, heat oil in a large nonstick skillet over medium heat. Add onion; cook 4 minutes or until tender, stirring frequently. Add garlic, oregano, and tomatoes; bring to a boil. Reduce heat, and simmer 6 minutes, stirring frequently. Stir in olives and capers; cook 1 minute. Spoon tomato mixture over fish. Sprinkle with chopped parsley, if desired. **YIELD:** 4 servings (serving size: 1 fillet, ³/₄ cup tomato mixture, and 1 tablespoon chopped parsley).

CALORIES 238; FAT 4.8g (sat 0.8g, mono 2.5g, poly 0.8g); PROTEIN 35.5g; CARB 12g; FIBER 1.5g; CHOL 63mg; IRON 2.4mg; SODIUM 736mg; CALC 142mg

GO GRILL

To avoid overcooking seafood, go with a medium-hot fire, and start checking the fish several minutes before you think that it's done. Test for flakiness with a fork, or make a small slit in the thickest part of the fish with a sharp knife. Cooked fish will be firm to the touch and opaque; undercooked fish will appear shiny and semitranslucent.

Maple-Glazed Salmon

Find ancho chile powder in the spice section of most supermarkets (substitute 2 teaspoons regular chili powder if needed). Round out the meal with a spring salad and small, steamed red potatoes.

2 teaspoons paprika	4 (6-ounce) salmon fillets
1 teaspoon chili powder	1 teaspoon sea or kosher salt
1 teaspoon ancho chile powder	Cooking spray
½ teaspoon ground cumin	1 teaspoon maple syrup
½ teaspoon brown sugar	

1. Prepare grill to medium heat.

2. Combine first 5 ingredients. Sprinkle fish with salt; rub with paprika mixture.

3. Place fish on grill rack coated with cooking spray; grill 7 minutes. Drizzle fish with syrup; grill 1 minute or until fish flakes easily when tested with a fork. **YIELD:** 4 servings (serving size: 1 salmon fillet).

CALORIES 286; FAT 13.5g (sat 3.2g, mono 5.7g, poly 3.4g); PROTEIN 36.5g; CARB 2.9g; FIBER 0.6g; CHOL 87mg; IRON 1.1mg; SODIUM 670mg; CALC 30mg

GO GRILL

Grill Fish

• When you grill seafood, it's particularly important that the rack be very clean. Any residue on the rack could interfere with the seafood's delicate flavor; a clean rack also helps prevent sticking.

• Lightly spray the grill rack with cooking spray before placing it over the coals. This keeps the food from sticking and makes the grill rack easier to clean.

• Always place seafood on a hot grill rack and leave it there for several minutes before you try to move it. This way, a sear will develop between the fish and the grill rack, which will further help to prevent sticking.

FISH THAT CAN TAKE THE HEAT

The most important thing to know when grilling fish is what kind to use. You want fish that has a thick, firm, meaty texture so that it won't fall apart while it's cooking. Although some firm-textured fish tend to be higher in fat than other, more delicate fish, it's the type of fat that's heart-healthy. Here are some of the fish that are well suited for the grill.

GROUPER: This white-meat fish is sold in fillets and steaks. If you can't find grouper, you can use sea bass or mahimahi.

HALIBUT: The meat of this fish is white and mild-flavored and comes in steaks and fillets. Although it's a firm fish, it's a tad more delicate than the other fish in this list, so be gentle when turning it on the grill.

SALMON: With a range of flavors from rich to mild, salmon can take on a char and still keep its distinct taste. Salmon's pink meat comes in steaks and fillets.

SWORDFISH: This mild but distinctive-tasting fish has firm, gray-white flesh and a meaty texture. Its natural oil content keeps it moist while grilling. You can usually find it sold as steaks.

TUNA: If you're new to grilling fish, fresh tuna is a good place to start. It cooks like a beefsteak, and its deep red meat almost never sticks to the grill.

202 calories

Veracruz-Style Red Snapper

Adding fresh cilantro and olives to bottled salsa and canned beans gives you fresh-from-the-garden-taste without much chopping. Feel free to use your favorite canned beans for variety. The salsa is also great with grilled chicken. Serve the snapper with steamed green beans and fruit tea.

4 (6-ounce) red snapper or tilapia fillets
Cooking spray
 ½ teaspoon ground cumin
 ¼ teaspoon salt
 ¼ teaspoon ground red pepper
 ¼ cup chopped fresh cilantro
 ¼ cup chopped pitted green olives
 ¼ cup bottled salsa
 1 (16-ounce) can pinto beans, drained
 1 (14.5-ounce) can diced tomatoes, drained
 4 lime wedges (optional)

1. Prepare grill or broiler.

2. Coat both sides of fillets with cooking spray; sprinkle with cumin, salt, and red pepper. Place fillets on grill rack or broiler pan coated with cooking spray; cook 5 minutes on each side or until fish flakes easily when tested with a fork.

3. Combine cilantro and next 4 ingredients. Serve fillets with salsa mixture and, if desired, lime wedges. **YIELD:** 4 servings (serving size: 1 fish fillet, ½ cup salsa, and 1 lime wedge).

CALORIES 202; FAT 3.2g (sat 0.5g, mono 1g, poly 1.2g); PROTEIN 28.2g; CARB 14.6g; FIBER 5.2g; CHOL 42mg; IRON 1.9mg; SODIUM 571mg; CALC 94mg

QUICK TIP: To chop cilantro quickly, wash and dry the entire bunch while it's still bound together. Starting at the top of the bunch, chop only the amount of cilantro leaves you need. (Don't worry about including the stems; they won't affect the flavor.) This method also works for parsley.

GO GRILL

MENU • *serves 4*

Veracruz-Style Red Snapper

Steamed green beans

Fruit tea
Combine 4 cups unsweetened tea with ½ cup raspberry or fruit-
flavored syrup (such as Torani) in a pitcher. Fill four tall glasses ¾ full
of ice; pour tea mixture over ice just before serving. Garnish with lime
wedges, if desired.

QUICK&EASY

Balsamic-Glazed Tuna

This dish is easy enough to make for a weeknight, yet more than appropriate for a special meal with company, too. Serve with couscous or sautéed zucchini.

Cooking spray
1¼ teaspoons coarsely ground black pepper
¼ teaspoon salt
4 (6-ounce) tuna steaks (about ¾ inch thick)
¼ cup fat-free, less-sodium chicken broth

1 tablespoon balsamic vinegar
4 teaspoons dark brown sugar
1 tablespoon low-sodium soy sauce
½ teaspoon cornstarch
¼ cup diagonally sliced green onions

1. Place a grill pan coated with cooking spray over medium-high heat until hot. Sprinkle pepper and salt over fish. Place fish in grill pan; cook 3 minutes on each side or until medium-rare or desired degree of doneness. Remove from heat.
2. Combine broth, vinegar, sugar, soy sauce, and cornstarch in a small saucepan. Bring to a boil; cook 1 minute, stirring constantly. Spoon glaze over fish; top with green onions. **YIELD:** 4 servings (serving size: 1 steak and 1 tablespoon glaze).

CALORIES 266; FAT 8.5g (sat 2.2g, mono 2.3g, poly 2.9g); PROTEIN 40.3g; CARB 4.6g; FIBER 0.3g; CHOL 65mg; IRON 2.2mg; SODIUM 366mg; CALC 11mg

CHOICE INGREDIENT: Balsamic vinegar has a pungent sweetness that adds a pleasant tang to vinaigrettes and sauces. Prices for balsamic vinegar vary greatly depending on the quality, but we recommend a middle-of-the-road variety for everyday use, such as Alessi's four-year balsamic vinegar.

GO GRILL

Buy and Cook Shellfish

To save prep time, instead of peeling and deveining your own shrimp, you can buy peeled and deveined raw shrimp at the seafood counter of most supermarkets. This chart shows how much peeled and deveined shrimp to buy when the recipe calls for unpeeled shrimp.

UNPEELED RAW SHRIMP		PEELED & DEVEINED RAW SHRIMP
⅔ pound	=	½ pound
1 pound	=	¾ pound
1⅓ pounds	=	1 pound
2 pounds	=	1½ pounds
2⅔ pounds	=	2 pounds
4 pounds	=	3 pounds

STORING AND USING FRESH SHRIMP

REFREEZING SHRIMP: Because most shrimp are quick-frozen at sea and then defrosted for sale, we often get asked if it's OK to refreeze them. We've done it for years without any problem so that we could store unused shrimp for later use. When you want to use your refrozen shrimp, just thaw them out in a bowl or sink filled with tap water.

DEVEINED SHRIMP: Most recipes call for shrimp to be peeled and deveined. However, except for the largest shrimp, there is neither danger nor distaste in leaving the thin black line (vein) right where it is. However, if you are butterflying your shrimp, deveining occurs anyway.

SHELLFISH: FISH THAT CAN TAKE THE HEAT

To prevent wooden skewers from burning while grilling, soak for 30 minutes in hot water beforehand.

SCALLOPS: This bivalve is usually classified into two groups: bay scallops and sea scallops. The larger sea scallops are best for grilling because, like shrimp, they have a meatier texture and can be easily skewered. They cook fast, though, so keep a close eye on them.

SHRIMP: Large shrimp are best for grilling. They can be easily skewered, and they cook quickly.

QUICK&**EASY**

Shrimp Saté with Pineapple Salsa

Buy peeled, cored fresh pineapple for the salsa. Enjoy the rest of it in a fresh fruit salad. If you are using wooden skewers, be sure to soak them in water for 30 minutes so that they won't burn on the grill. Complete the meal with lemony broccoli and white wine.

Salsa:
- ³/₄ cup finely chopped pineapple
- ¹/₄ cup finely chopped red onion
- 1 tablespoon minced seeded jalapeño pepper
- 1 tablespoon chopped fresh cilantro
- 1 tablespoon cider vinegar
- 1 teaspoon honey

Saté:
- 2 tablespoons chopped fresh mint
- 2 tablespoons fresh lime juice
- ¹/₄ teaspoon salt
- ¹/₄ teaspoon chili powder
- 24 large shrimp, peeled and deveined (about 1¹/₂ pounds)
- Cooking spray
- 4 cilantro sprigs (optional)

1. Prepare grill.
2. To prepare salsa, combine first 6 ingredients in a medium bowl.
3. To prepare saté, combine mint, juice, salt, and chili powder in a large bowl; add shrimp, tossing gently to coat. Thread 3 shrimp onto each of 8 (6-inch) skewers. Place shrimp on grill rack coated with cooking spray; grill 1¹/₂ minutes on each side or until shrimp turn pink. Serve with salsa. Garnish with cilantro sprigs, if desired.
YIELD: 4 servings (serving size: 2 skewers and ¹/₄ cup salsa).

CALORIES 208; FAT 3g (sat 0.6g, mono 0.4g, poly 1.2g); PROTEIN 34.9g; CARB 8.7g; FIBER 0.7g; CHOL 259mg; IRON 4.3mg; SODIUM 403mg; CALC 98mg

GO GRILL

Shrimp Saté with Pineapple Salsa

Lemony broccoli
Cook 1 (12-ounce) package broccoli florets in boiling water 3 minutes or until crisp-tender; drain. Place broccoli in a large bowl. Add 2 teaspoons fresh lemon juice, 2 teaspoons butter, ¼ teaspoon salt, and ¼ teaspoon pepper. Toss gently to coat.

White wine

TASTY ADDITIONS:
Dijon-Garlic Shrimp Glaze

Add a bit of zing to your grilled shrimp with this quick and tasty brush-on sauce. This tangy mixture adds just enough flavor to liven up shrimp, while still letting its natural sweetness shine.

3 tablespoons Dijon mustard   **2 tablespoons honey**

¼ cup fresh lemon juice   **2 garlic cloves, minced**

Start with 1½ pounds of large shrimp, peeled and deveined. Combine above ingredients, and stir with a whisk. Brush one side of shrimp with mixture. Grill for 1 to 2 minutes. Turn shrimp, brush with glaze, and cook 2 minutes or until shrimp are done. **SERVES 4.**

350-CALORIE
Soups, Salads, & Sandwiches

The Weeknight Pantry

A well-stocked pantry is the key to creating quick and healthful meals.

WITH THESE INGREDIENTS ON HAND, you'll always be able to get a tasty, healthful meal on the table without having to settle for just so-so dishes.

Pantry Basics

Broth
- ❑ beef
- ❑ chicken
- ❑ vegetable

Canned beans
- ❑ black
- ❑ cannellini
- ❑ garbanzo
- ❑ great Northern
- ❑ pinto

- ❑ Canned salmon
- ❑ Canned or packaged tuna
- ❑ Cornmeal

Grains
- ❑ barley
- ❑ bulgur
- ❑ millet
- ❑ quinoa

- ❑ Grits or polenta

Pastas
- ❑ couscous
- ❑ penne
- ❑ spaghetti

- ❑ Pasta sauce

Rice
- ❑ Arborio
- ❑ basmati
- ❑ jasmine
- ❑ white
- ❑ wild

- ❑ Tomato products, canned

Condiments
- ❑ Anchovy paste
- ❑ Bottled roasted red bell peppers
- ❑ Capers
- ❑ Chili paste
- ❑ Chipotle chiles in adobo sauce
- ❑ Chutneys
- ❑ Curry paste
- ❑ Dried herbs and spices
- ❑ Fresh garlic
- ❑ Jams
- ❑ Jellies

Mustards
- ❑ Dijon
- ❑ honey
- ❑ stone-ground

Oil
- ❑ canola
- ❑ dark sesame
- ❑ olive

- ❑ Peanut butter
- ❑ Raisins
- ❑ Salsa

Sauces
- ❑ fish
- ❑ hoisin
- ❑ low-sodium soy
- ❑ oyster sauce

- ❑ Seasoning blends
- ❑ Sun-dried tomatoes

Vinegars
- ❑ balsamic
- ❑ cider

- ❑ red wine
- ❑ rice
- ❑ sherry
- ❑ white wine

Wines
- ❑ red
- ❑ sherry
- ❑ white

Sweets
- ❑ Cocoa
- ❑ Honey
- ❑ Maple syrup
- ❑ Molasses
- ❑ Semisweet chocolate

Sugars
- ❑ brown
- ❑ granulated
- ❑ powdered
- ❑ turbinado

Refrigerator/ Freezer

Beef
- ❑ ground
- ❑ roasts
- ❑ steaks
- ❑ tenderloin

- ❑ Butter

Cheeses
- ❑ blue
- ❑ feta
- ❑ mozzarella
- ❑ Parmesan
- ❑ Romano

Chicken
- ❑ rotisserie
- ❑ skinless breast halves
- ❑ thighs

- ❑ Eggs
- ❑ Egg substitute

Fresh chiles
- ❑ jalapeño
- ❑ serrano

Fresh or frozen fish and shellfish
- ❑ salmon
- ❑ shrimp

- ❑ Fresh herbs
- ❑ Lemons
- ❑ Limes
- ❑ Oranges

Nuts
- ❑ almonds
- ❑ hazelnuts
- ❑ pecans
- ❑ pine nuts
- ❑ walnuts

Olives
- ❑ black
- ❑ green
- ❑ kalamata
- ❑ niçoise

- ❑ Pork tenderloin
- ❑ Salad dressings

Tofu
- ❑ firm
- ❑ soft

- ❑ Tubes of polenta
- ❑ Vegetables, frozen

Avocado Soup with Citrus-Shrimp Relish

This lovely no-cook soup makes a refreshing entrée when paired with a green salad.

Relish:
- 2 tablespoons chopped fresh cilantro
- 1 teaspoon grated lemon rind
- 1 teaspoon finely chopped red onion
- 1 teaspoon extra-virgin olive oil
- 8 ounces peeled and deveined medium shrimp, steamed and coarsely chopped

Soup:
- 2 cups fat-free, less-sodium chicken broth
- 1¾ cups chopped avocado (about 2)
- 1 cup water
- 1 cup rinsed and drained canned navy beans
- ½ cup fat-free plain yogurt
- 1½ tablespoons fresh lemon juice
- ¼ teaspoon salt
- ¼ teaspoon black pepper
- ¼ teaspoon hot pepper sauce (such as Tabasco)
- 1 small jalapeño pepper, seeded and chopped
- ¼ cup (1 ounce) crumbled queso fresco

1. To prepare relish, combine cilantro and next 4 ingredients in a small bowl, tossing gently.

2. To prepare soup, combine broth and next 9 ingredients in a blender; process until smooth, scraping sides. Ladle 1¼ cups avocado mixture into each of 4 bowls; top each serving with ¼ cup shrimp mixture and 1 tablespoon cheese. **YIELD:** 4 servings (serving size: 1¼ cups soup, ¼ cup shrimp mixture, and 1 tablespoon cheese).

CALORIES 292; FAT 13.2g (sat 2.2g, mono 7.8g, poly 2.6g); PROTEIN 23.9g; CARB 22.5g; FIBER 7.3g; CHOL 118mg; IRON 3.4mg; SODIUM 832mg; CALC 146mg

Sausage and Spinach Soup

Add fresh herbs after the soup cooks so that they'll retain their bright color and flavor. You can substitute 1 teaspoon dried herbs for each tablespoon fresh, but add them with the tomatoes. Serve with a toasted baguette.

10 ounces sweet turkey Italian sausage
Cooking spray
1 cup prechopped onion
2 teaspoons bottled minced garlic
$\frac{1}{2}$ cup water
1 (15-ounce) can cannellini beans, rinsed and drained
1 (14.5-ounce) can organic stewed tomatoes, undrained (such as Muir Glen)

1 (14-ounce) can fat-free, less-sodium chicken broth
2 cups baby spinach
1 tablespoon chopped fresh basil
2 teaspoons chopped fresh oregano
2 tablespoons grated fresh Romano cheese

1. Remove casings from sausage. Cook sausage in a large saucepan coated with cooking spray over high heat until browned, stirring to crumble. Add onion and garlic to pan; cook 2 minutes. Stir in $\frac{1}{2}$ cup water, beans, tomatoes, and broth. Cover and bring to a boil. Uncover and cook 3 minutes or until slightly thick. Remove from heat, and stir in spinach, basil, and oregano. Ladle $1\frac{1}{2}$ cups soup into each of 4 bowls, and sprinkle each serving with $1\frac{1}{2}$ teaspoons cheese. **YIELD:** 4 servings (serving size: $1\frac{1}{2}$ cups soup and $1\frac{1}{2}$ teaspoons cheese).

CALORIES 261; FAT 8.6g (sat 2.8g, mono 2.7g, poly 2.5g); PROTEIN 20.9g; CARB 23.1g; FIBER 5.4g; CHOL 62mg; IRON 3.4mg; SODIUM 842mg; CALC 105mg

261
calories

310
calories

Southwestern Pork Soup

Substitute chicken for pork in this dish, if you prefer. Pink beans
are similar to pinto beans but smaller; if you can't find pink
beans, substitute pintos. Add cheddar corn bread and orange
slices to round out the meal.

Cooking spray
1 cup prechopped onion
²/₃ cup prechopped green bell
pepper
1 tablespoon bottled minced
garlic
1 jalapeño pepper, seeded and
minced
1 pound pork tenderloin,
trimmed and cut into bite-sized
pieces
2 cups fat-free, less-sodium
chicken broth

2 teaspoons chili powder
1 teaspoon ground cumin
¹/₂ teaspoon salt
¹/₄ teaspoon black pepper
1 (15-ounce) can pink beans,
rinsed and drained
1 (14-ounce) can diced tomatoes,
undrained
2 tablespoons chopped fresh
cilantro
1 cup diced avocado

1. Heat a small nonstick Dutch oven over medium heat. Coat pan
with cooking spray. Add onion, bell pepper, garlic, and jalapeño
to pan; sauté 2 minutes. Add pork; cook 3 minutes. Add broth and
next 6 ingredients; bring to a boil. Partially cover, reduce heat,
and simmer 6 minutes or until pork is done, stirring occasionally.
Remove from heat, and stir in cilantro. Serve with avocado. **YIELD:**
4 servings (serving size: about 1³/₄ cups soup and ¹/₄ cup avocado).

CALORIES 310; FAT 10.5g (sat 2.4g, mono 5.5g, poly 1.4g); PROTEIN 30.6g; CARB 24.5g; FIBER 8.3g; CHOL 74mg;
IRON 3.7mg; SODIUM 911mg; CALC 82mg

Three-Bean Chili

Purchase corn muffins from the supermarket to round out this heart-healthy dinner.

2 teaspoons olive oil
1 cup prechopped onion
$1/2$ cup prechopped green bell pepper
2 teaspoons bottled minced garlic
$3/4$ cup water
2 tablespoons tomato paste
2 teaspoons chili powder
2 teaspoons ground cumin
$1/4$ teaspoon black pepper
1 ($15^1/2$-ounce) can garbanzo beans, rinsed and drained
1 ($15^1/2$-ounce) can red kidney beans, rinsed and drained
1 ($15^1/2$-ounce) can black beans, rinsed and drained
1 ($14^1/2$-ounce) can organic vegetable broth (such as Swanson Certified Organic)
1 ($14^1/2$-ounce) can no-salt-added diced tomatoes, undrained
1 tablespoon yellow cornmeal
$1/4$ cup chopped fresh cilantro
6 tablespoons reduced-fat sour cream

1. Heat oil in a large saucepan over medium-high heat. Add onion, bell pepper, and garlic to pan; sauté 3 minutes. Stir in $3/4$ cup water and next 9 ingredients; bring to a boil. Reduce heat, and simmer 8 minutes. Stir in cornmeal; cook 2 minutes. Remove from heat; stir in cilantro. Serve with sour cream. **YIELD:** 6 servings (serving size: $1^1/3$ cups chili and 1 tablespoon sour cream).

CALORIES 180; FAT 4.9g (sat 1.5g, mono 1.7g, poly 0.3g); PROTEIN 8.4g; CARB 29.5g; FIBER 8.6g; CHOL 5mg; IRON 2.3mg; SODIUM 714mg; CALC 86mg

180
calories

212
calories

Quick Fall Minestrone

Make the most of fall produce such as butternut squash and kale in this hearty vegetarian soup. Pasta and beans make it especially filling.

1 tablespoon canola oil
1 cup chopped onion
2 garlic cloves, minced
6 cups vegetable broth (such as Swanson Certified Organic)
2½ cups (¾-inch) cubed peeled butternut squash
2½ cups (¾-inch) cubed peeled baking potato
1 cup (1-inch) cut green beans (about ¼ pound)
½ cup chopped carrot
1 teaspoon dried oregano
½ teaspoon freshly ground black pepper
¼ teaspoon salt
4 cups chopped kale
½ cup uncooked orzo (rice-shaped pasta)
1 (16-ounce) can cannellini beans or other white beans, rinsed and drained
½ cup (2 ounces) grated fresh Parmesan cheese

1. Heat oil in a large Dutch oven over medium-high heat. Add onion and garlic; sauté 2½ minutes or until tender. Add broth and next 7 ingredients; bring to a boil. Reduce heat, and simmer 3 minutes. Add kale, orzo, and beans; cook 5 minutes or until orzo is done and vegetables are tender. Sprinkle with cheese. **YIELD:** 8 servings (serving size: 1½ cups soup and 1 tablespoon cheese).

CALORIES 212; FAT 5g (sat 1.6g, mono 1g, poly 1.2g); PROTEIN 9.6g; CARB 36g; FIBER 3.9g; CHOL 5mg; IRON 1.9mg; SODIUM 961mg; CALC 164mg

QUICK TIP: To remove the skin from the squash quickly, use a vegetable peeler.

Quick Fall Minestrone

Monterey Jack and roasted red-pepper quesadillas
Preheat broiler. Place 8 (6-inch) fat-free flour tortillas on a large baking sheet coated with cooking spray. Sprinkle each tortilla evenly with 2 tablespoons shredded Monterey Jack cheese and 2 tablespoons chopped bottled roasted red bell peppers. Top each prepared tortilla with another (6-inch) fat-free flour tortilla; coat tops with cooking spray. Broil 3 minutes or until lightly browned. Carefully turn over; coat tops with cooking spray. Broil an additional 3 minutes or until lightly browned. Cut each quesadilla into 4 wedges; serve 4 wedges per person.

Cantaloupe, grape, and honeydew fruit salad

Pasta Fagioli Soup

This Italian soup derives its name—*fagioli*—and its high-fiber content from kidney beans. Serve with crusty Italian bread and a Caesar salad for a quick weeknight supper.

12 ounces Santa Fe chicken sausage, halved lengthwise and sliced (such as Amy's)

3 cups fat-free, less-sodium chicken broth

½ cup uncooked small seashell pasta

2 cups coarsely chopped zucchini (about 2 small zucchini)

1 (14.5-ounce) can stewed tomatoes, undrained

1 teaspoon dried basil

1 teaspoon dried oregano

1 (15-ounce) can kidney beans, rinsed and drained

⅓ cup (about 1½ ounces) shredded Asiago cheese

1. Heat a large saucepan over high heat. Add sausage; cook 2 minutes, stirring constantly. Add broth and pasta; bring to a boil. Cover, reduce heat, and simmer 4 minutes. Add zucchini and tomatoes; bring to a boil. Cover, reduce heat, and simmer 2 minutes. Stir in basil, oregano, and beans; cover and simmer 3 minutes or until pasta and zucchini are tender. Sprinkle with cheese. **YIELD:** 5 servings (serving size: about 1⅓ cups soup and about 1 tablespoon Asiago cheese).

CALORIES 319; FAT 9.2g (sat 3.3g, mono 3.8g, poly 0.8g); PROTEIN 21.9g; CARB 39.7g; FIBER 9.6g; CHOL 56mg; IRON 4.4mg; SODIUM 858mg; CALC 56mg

319
calories

KITCHEN HOW-TO
Build a Healthful Salad

GREENS Most leafy greens contribute folate, the B vitamin critical to red blood cell health and the reduction of neural tube birth defects such as spina bifida. Also, they provide generous amounts of vitamin A and the antioxidants lutein and zeaxanthin, which may help protect against macular degeneration.

FRUITS All fruits provide abundant good nutrients (vitamin C and potassium, in particular) and a laundry list of disease-fighting chemicals in a package that's naturally low in fat, sodium, and calories. Blueberries contain polyphenol (a phytochemical linked to heart disease and cancer prevention) compounds called anthocyanins and proanthocyanins that may play a role in preserving memory. Grapes also offer polyphenols.

NUTS AND SEEDS One-fourth cup of nuts or seeds adds nearly 5 grams of high-quality protein, as well as generous amounts of vitamin E, fiber, minerals, and arginine, a compound that helps blood vessels to function. Nuts are high in fat—the healthful, unsaturated kind.

TOMATOES With plenty of vitamin C, some blood pressure-lowering potassium, and folate, tomatoes also impart the plant chemicals flavonoids (potential cancer fighters) and phytosterols (which may help lower cholesterol).

ONIONS Onions are plentiful sources of disease-fighting phenols and flavonoids, both potential cancer fighters and weapons against some chronic diseases. The richer its phenolic and flavonoid content, the better an onion's protective effect, according to Rui Hai Liu, MD, PhD, an associate professor of food science at Cornell University.

VEGETABLE OILS Liquid vegetable oils are rich in vitamin E and unsaturated fats (monounsaturated and polyunsaturated), which don't clog arteries. Olive oil is particularly rich in phenol antioxidants.

SEAFOOD AND OTHER PROTEINS Fatty fish such as salmon or tuna offer omega-3 fats, which help lower the risk for heart disease. The American Heart Association suggests eating at least two 3-ounce cooked servings of fish per week.

Thai Beef Salad

313 calories

1 cup loosely packed fresh cilantro leaves

¼ cup fresh lime juice (about 3 limes)

2 tablespoons low-sodium soy sauce

1½ tablespoons Thai fish sauce

1 tablespoon honey

2 teaspoons grated orange rind

2 garlic cloves, peeled

½ small serrano chile

2 teaspoons olive oil

4 (4-ounce) beef tenderloin steaks, trimmed

¼ teaspoon black pepper

⅛ teaspoon salt

2 cups shredded Napa cabbage

1 cup grated, seeded, peeled cucumber

⅓ cup thinly sliced green onions

3 tablespoons chopped fresh basil

1 (12-ounce) package broccoli coleslaw

1 (11-ounce) can mandarin oranges in light syrup, drained

1. Place first 8 ingredients in a food processor; process until smooth.

2. Heat oil in a large nonstick skillet over medium-high heat. Sprinkle steak evenly on both sides with pepper and salt. Add steak to pan; cook 4 minutes on each side or until desired degree of doneness. Remove steak from pan; let stand 5 minutes. Cut into thin slices.

3. Combine cabbage and remaining 5 ingredients in a large bowl. Drizzle slaw mixture with cilantro mixture; toss. Arrange 2 cups slaw mixture on each of 4 plates; top each serving with 3 ounces beef. **YIELD:** 4 servings (serving size: 2 cups slaw and 3 ounces beef).

CALORIES 313; FAT 11.8g (sat 4g, mono 5.5g, poly 0.6g); PROTEIN 28.2g; CARB 22.6g; FIBER 5g; CHOL 71mg; IRON 2.8mg; SODIUM 883mg; CALC 105mg

If you want a salad with beef but are trying to limit your calorie intake, this is the salad for you. Not only is it ideal for a health-conscious meal, it also boasts excellent flavor and can be on the table in about 20 minutes.

QUICK&EASY

Chicken Cobb Salad

Bacon, blue cheese, avocado, and chicken are all ingredients in the classic Cobb salad. Serve with a chilled summer soup for a light and refreshing meal.

Cooking spray

- 1½ pounds skinless, boneless chicken breast cutlets
- ¼ teaspoon salt
- ¼ teaspoon black pepper
- 8 cups mixed greens
- 1 cup cherry tomatoes, halved
- ⅓ cup diced peeled avocado
- 2 tablespoons sliced green onions
- ⅓ cup fat-free Italian dressing
- 2 tablespoons crumbled blue cheese
- 1 bacon slice, cooked and crumbled

1. Heat a large nonstick skillet over medium-high heat. Coat pan with cooking spray. Sprinkle chicken with salt and pepper. Add chicken to pan; cook 5 minutes on each side or until done. Cut into ½-inch slices.

2. Combine greens, tomatoes, avocado, and onions in a large bowl. Drizzle greens mixture with dressing; toss gently to coat. Arrange about 2 cups greens mixture on each of 4 salad plates. Top each serving with 4 ounces chicken, 1½ teaspoons cheese, and about ½ teaspoon bacon. **YIELD:** 4 servings (serving size: 2 cups greens, 4 ounces chicken, 1½ teaspoons cheese, and about ½ teaspoon bacon).

CALORIES 263; FAT 8g (sat 2.4g, mono 3.2g, poly 1.4g); PROTEIN 37.9g; CARB 8.9g; FIBER 3.7g; CHOL 99mg; IRON 2.6mg; SODIUM 606mg; CALC 89mg

Soba Noodle Salad with Seared Tuna

Look for Japanese soba noodles in the ethnic-food section of your supermarket.

6	ounces uncooked soba (buckwheat noodles)	¼	cup finely chopped green onions
	Cooking spray	3	tablespoons rice vinegar
1	(1-pound) sushi-grade tuna steak	2	tablespoons low-sodium soy sauce
½	teaspoon salt, divided	1	tablespoon peanut oil
¼	teaspoon freshly ground black pepper	1½	teaspoons dark sesame oil
1	cup finely chopped English cucumber	1	teaspoon sugar
1	cup shredded carrot	½	teaspoon crushed red pepper
½	cup julienne-cut radishes	2	tablespoons sesame seeds, toasted
⅓	cup finely chopped red bell pepper		

1. Cook noodles according to package directions; drain and rinse with cold water. Drain; set aside.

2. Heat a large nonstick skillet over medium-high heat. Coat pan with cooking spray. Sprinkle both sides of tuna with ¼ teaspoon salt and black pepper. Place tuna in pan, and cook 3 minutes on each side or until desired degree of doneness. Transfer to a platter; cool slightly. Cut tuna into 6 equal pieces.

3. Combine noodles, ¼ teaspoon salt, cucumber, and next 10 ingredients in a large bowl; toss well to combine. Arrange 1 cup noodle mixture on each of 6 plates. Top each serving with 1 teaspoon sesame seeds and 1 tuna piece. **YIELD:** 6 servings.

CALORIES 256; FAT 6.3g (sat 1g, mono 2.6g, poly 2.5g); PROTEIN 22g; CARB 28.2g; FIBER 2.9g; CHOL 34mg; IRON 1.9mg; SODIUM 570mg; CALC 62mg

256
calories

149

Chickpea-Vegetable Salad with Curried Yogurt Dressing

337 calories

Dressing:
- ¹/₃ cup chopped fresh cilantro
- 2 tablespoons olive oil
- 1 tablespoon lemon juice
- 1¹/₂ teaspoons curry powder
- ³/₄ teaspoon salt
- ¹/₂ teaspoon bottled minced garlic
- ¹/₄ teaspoon freshly ground black pepper
- 1 (8-ounce) carton plain fat-free yogurt

Salad:
- 2 cups finely shredded carrot
- 1¹/₂ cups thinly sliced yellow or red bell pepper
- 1¹/₂ cups chopped plum tomato
- ¹/₂ cup golden raisins
- ¹/₄ cup finely chopped red onion
- 2 (15¹/₂-ounce) cans chickpeas (garbanzo beans), drained
- 12 cups chopped romaine lettuce

1. To prepare dressing, combine first 8 ingredients in a small bowl; stir mixture with a whisk.

2. To prepare salad, combine carrot and next 5 ingredients in a large bowl. Pour ¹/₂ cup dressing over carrot mixture, tossing gently to coat. Place 2 cups lettuce on each of 6 plates, and drizzle each serving with about 1 tablespoon dressing. Top each serving with 1¹/₃ cups carrot mixture. **YIELD:** 6 servings (serving size: 2 cups lettuce, 1 tablespoon dressing, and 1¹/₃ cups carrot mixture).

CALORIES 337; FAT 8g (sat 1.1g, mono 4.1g, poly 2g); PROTEIN 15.4g; CARB 55.4g; FIBER 8.9g; CHOL 1mg; IRON 5.7mg; SODIUM 573mg; CALC 201mg

QUICK TIP: To cut prep time, pick up packages of shredded carrots and torn romaine lettuce in the produce section of your market. In addition, if you are preparing the menu suggested on page 151, we recommend preparing the dressing and salad ingredients while the pita toasts.

Chickpea-Vegetable Salad with Curried Yogurt Dressing

Spiced pita wedges

Combine 1 tablespoon melted butter and ¼ teaspoon each of coriander, cumin, and turmeric. Brush evenly over rough sides of an 8-inch split pita. Cut each pita half into 6 wedges; place on a baking sheet. Bake at 350° for 12 minutes or until toasted.

Quick Taco Salad

332 calories

12 ounces ground round
2 cups chopped yellow, red, or green bell pepper
2 cups bottled salsa
¼ cup chopped fresh cilantro
4 cups coarsely chopped romaine lettuce

2 cups chopped plum tomato
1 cup (4 ounces) shredded reduced-fat sharp Cheddar cheese
1 cup crumbled baked tortilla chips (about 12 chips)
¼ cup chopped green onions

1. Cook beef and bell pepper in a large nonstick skillet over medium-high heat until beef is browned; stir to crumble. Add salsa; bring to a boil. Stir in cilantro; keep warm.

2. Place 1 cup lettuce on each of 4 plates; top each with 1 cup meat mixture. Sprinkle each serving with ½ cup tomato, ¼ cup cheese, ¼ cup chips, and 1 tablespoon onions. **YIELD:** 4 servings (serving size: 1 cup lettuce, 1 cup meat mixture, ½ cup tomato, ¼ cup cheese, ¼ cup chips, and 1 tablespoon onions).

CALORIES 332; FAT 11.1g (sat 4.8g, mono 3.5g, poly 0.9g); PROTEIN 32g; CARB 28.5g; FIBER 6.3g; CHOL 68mg; IRON 5.6mg; SODIUM 908mg; CALC 348mg

SOUPS, SALADS, & SANDWICHES

5-Ingredient Weeknight Salads

Create a new salad for each weeknight meal with only 5 ingredients.

GROCERY LIST

- Red leaf lettuce (2 heads)
- Cucumbers (5)
- Plum tomatoes (11)
- Reduced-fat olive oil vinaigrette (2 bottles)
- Freshly ground pepper (optional)
- Feta cheese (4-ounce package)

TOSSED SALAD Combine 4 cups torn lettuce; ½ cucumber, chopped; 3 tomatoes, sliced; and ¼ cup vinaigrette. Toss. Sprinkle each serving with 1 tablespoon crumbled feta cheese and freshly ground pepper. **Yield:** 4 servings.

CALORIES 71; FAT 5.2g (sat 1.7g, mono 0.5g, poly 0.1g); PROTEIN 2.5g; CARB 5.1g; FIBER 1.2g; CHOL 8mg; IRON 0.7mg; SODIUM 234mg; CALC 68mg

MARINATED CUCUMBERS AND TOMATOES Combine 2 cucumbers, thinly sliced; 4 tomatoes, sliced; and ½ cup vinaigrette. Cover and chill. Sprinkle with freshly ground pepper, if desired. **Yield:** 4 servings.

CALORIES 86; FAT 6.1g (sat 0.5g, mono 0.0g, poly 0.1g); PROTEIN 2.1g; CARB 8.5g; FIBER 2.3g; CHOL 0mg; IRON 0.7mg; SODIUM 243mg; CALC 37mg

MARINATED TOMATOES Combine 4 tomatoes, sliced, and ¼ cup vinaigrette. Cover and chill. Sprinkle each serving with 1 tablespoon crumbled feta cheese; sprinkle with freshly ground pepper, if desired. **Yield:** 4 servings.

CALORIES 66; FAT 5.1g (sat 1.7g, mono 0.5g, poly 0.1g); PROTEIN 1.9g; CARB 4.3g; FIBER 0.7g; CHOL 8mg; IRON 0.2mg; SODIUM 228mg; CALC 52mg

SIMPLY GREENS Combine 8 cups torn lettuce and ¼ cup vinaigrette; toss. Sprinkle each serving with 1 tablespoon crumbled feta cheese and freshly ground pepper. **Yield:** 4 (2-cup) servings.

CALORIES 64; FAT 5.1g (sat 1.7g, mono 0.4g, poly 0.1g); PROTEIN 2.1g; CARB 3.2g; FIBER 0.5g; CHOL 8mg; IRON 0.7mg; SODIUM 239mg; CALC 65mg

MARINATED CUCUMBERS WITH FETA Combine 2 cucumbers, thinly sliced, and ¼ cup vinaigrette. Cover and chill. Sprinkle each serving with 1 tablespoon crumbled feta cheese. **Yield:** 4 servings.

CALORIES 70; FAT 4.9g (sat 1.7g, mono 0.4g, poly 0.1g); PROTEIN 2.9g; CARB 4.9g; FIBER 1.5g; CHOL 8mg; IRON 0.6mg; SODIUM 225mg; CALC 77mg

Tuscan Tuna Sandwiches

Chopped fennel bulb, fresh basil, and capers lend this speedy supper vibrant Italian flair. Toasted bread adds texture, but it's an optional step. You can serve the sandwich with baked potato chips.

¼ cup finely chopped fennel bulb
¼ cup prechopped red onion
¼ cup chopped fresh basil
2 tablespoons drained capers
2 tablespoons fresh lemon juice
2 tablespoons extra-virgin olive oil
¼ teaspoon black pepper

2 (6-ounce) cans solid white tuna in water, drained
1 (4-ounce) jar chopped roasted red bell peppers, drained
8 (1-ounce) slices sourdough bread, toasted

1. Combine first 9 ingredients in a bowl, stirring well. Spoon ½ cup tuna mixture on each of 4 bread slices. Top each serving with 1 bread slice. Cut each sandwich in half diagonally. **YIELD:** 4 servings (serving size: 1 sandwich).

CALORIES 292; FAT 10g (sat 1.6g, mono 5.6g, poly 1.7g); PROTEIN 25.2g; CARB 24.3g; FIBER 3.3g; CHOL 36mg; IRON 2.4mg; SODIUM 878mg; CALC 85mg

DRESSING UP SANDWICHES

• Instead of iceberg lettuce, try using greens such as peppery endive, colorful radicchio, baby spinach leaves, or arugula.

• Spread your bread with prepared pesto, olive tapenade, honey mustard, or cream cheese mixed with fresh herbs.

• Add extra flavor with jarred roasted red peppers, pepperoncini peppers, sweet and hot jalapeños, rehydrated sun-dried tomatoes, grilled pineapple slices, or grilled avocado slices.

• Use hearty or flavored breads, and toast them first so that they'll stand up to the ingredients.

292
calories

Onion-Smothered Italian Burgers

Serve corn on the cob as a quick and easy side dish and low-fat strawberry ice cream for dessert.

1 teaspoon olive oil
2 cups thinly sliced Vidalia or other sweet onion
2 teaspoons sugar
¼ teaspoon salt
⅛ teaspoon black pepper
1 tablespoon balsamic vinegar
3 tablespoons preshredded fresh Parmesan cheese
2 tablespoons tomato paste
1 teaspoon dried oregano
½ teaspoon garlic powder
¼ teaspoon dried basil
1 pound extra-lean ground beef
Cooking spray
4 (1½-ounce) hamburger buns

1. Heat oil in a large nonstick skillet over medium-high heat. Add onion and next 3 ingredients to pan. Cook 6 minutes or until lightly browned, stirring occasionally. Add vinegar to pan; cook 30 seconds, stirring constantly. Remove from heat; keep warm.
2. Combine cheese and next 5 ingredients in a medium bowl; shape meat mixture into 4 (3-inch) patties. Heat a grill pan over medium-high heat. Coat pan with cooking spray. Add patties to pan. Cook 5 minutes on each side or until desired degree of doneness. Place 1 patty on bottom half of each bun; top each patty with ¼ cup onion mixture and top half of a bun. **YIELD:** 4 servings (serving size: 1 burger).

CALORIES 330; FAT 8.9g (sat 3g, mono 3.7g, poly 1.5g); PROTEIN 28.9g; CARB 33.7g; FIBER 2.9g; CHOL 65mg; IRON 4mg; SODIUM 541mg; CALC 142mg

The patty melt gets a makeover with ground turkey, but substitute ground chicken or ground sirloin, if you prefer. Pair sandwiches with vegetable chips.

Open-Faced Turkey Patty Melt

348 calories

1 teaspoon olive oil
1 cup vertically sliced Vidalia or other sweet onion
¼ cup part-skim ricotta cheese
1½ teaspoons Worcestershire sauce
½ teaspoon black pepper
1 pound ground turkey breast

1 large egg white, lightly beaten
Cooking spray
4 (1-ounce) slices reduced-fat Swiss cheese
4 slices light rye bread
¼ cup country-style Dijon mustard

1. Heat oil in a large nonstick skillet over medium heat. Add onion to pan. Cook 5 minutes or until lightly browned; stir occasionally. Transfer onion to a bowl.

2. Preheat broiler.

3. Combine cheese and next 4 ingredients. Divide turkey mixture into 4 equal portions, shaping each into a ½-inch-thick patty. Return pan to medium heat. Coat pan with cooking spray. Add patties to pan; cook 4 minutes or until brown. Turn patties over; cook 1 minute. Top each patty with 1 cheese slice; cook 3 minutes or until cheese melts and patties are done.

4. Place bread slices in a single layer on a baking sheet; broil 2 minutes or until toasted. Spread 1 tablespoon mustard on each bread slice; top each serving with 1 patty. Divide onion mixture evenly among sandwiches. **YIELD:** 4 servings (serving size: 1 sandwich).

CALORIES 348; FAT 9g (sat 4g, mono 2.2g, poly 2.6g); PROTEIN 43.4g; CARB 22.4g; FIBER 1.5g; CHOL 50mg; IRON 2.1mg; SODIUM 848mg; CALC 325mg

Cashew Chicken Salad Sandwiches

This goes together as fast as an ordinary turkey sandwich but is much more interesting. Add lettuce and tomato, if you'd like. Serve with sliced fresh fruit for a casual dinner for two.

¼ cup fat-free sour cream
1 tablespoon light mayonnaise
¼ teaspoon curry powder
2 cups chopped roasted skinless, boneless chicken breasts (about 2 breasts)
⅓ cup chopped celery
2 tablespoons chopped dry-roasted cashews

1 tablespoon finely chopped green onions
2 (2-ounce) whole-wheat hamburger buns
Lettuce (optional)
Tomato (optional)

1. Combine first 3 ingredients in a large bowl, stirring until well blended. Add chicken, celery, cashews, and green onions; stir well. Serve chicken salad on buns. **YIELD:** 2 servings (serving size: ⅔ cup chicken salad and 1 bun).

CALORIES 350; FAT 10.3g (sat 2.6g, mono 1.5g, poly 1.8g); PROTEIN 31.6g; CARB 35.8g; FIBER 4.8g; CHOL 69mg; IRON 1.8mg; SODIUM 925mg; CALC 115mg

QUICK&EASY

Portobello Cheeseburgers

Portobello mushrooms are well-paired with pungent Gorgonzola cheese. Buy this blue cheese already crumbled to save more time.

2 teaspoons olive oil
4 (4-inch) portobello caps
¼ teaspoon salt
¼ teaspoon black pepper
1 tablespoon bottled minced garlic
¼ cup (1 ounce) crumbled Gorgonzola cheese

3 tablespoons reduced-fat mayonnaise
4 (2-ounce) sandwich rolls
2 cups trimmed arugula
½ cup sliced bottled roasted red bell peppers

1. Heat oil in a large nonstick skillet over medium-high heat. Sprinkle mushrooms with salt and black pepper. Add mushrooms to pan; sauté 4 minutes or until tender, turning once. Add garlic to pan; sauté 30 seconds. Remove mushroom mixture from heat.
2. Combine cheese and mayonnaise, stirring well. Spread about 2 tablespoons mayonnaise mixture over bottom half of each roll; top each serving with ½ cup arugula and 2 tablespoons bell peppers. Place 1 mushroom on each serving, and top with top halves of rolls. **YIELD:** 4 servings (serving size: 1 burger).

CALORIES 278; FAT 9.9g (sat 3g, mono 1.7g, poly 0.4g); PROTEIN 9.3g; CARB 33.7g; FIBER 2.4g; CHOL 6mg; IRON 1.7mg; SODIUM 726mg; CALC 129mg

SOUPS, SALADS, & SANDWICHES

Portobello Cheeseburgers

Oven fries with aioli
Preheat oven to 400°. Cut 2 pounds peeled baking potatoes into
¼-inch-thick strips. Place potatoes on a jelly-roll pan. Drizzle with
1 tablespoon canola oil and sprinkle with ½ teaspoon salt; toss to
coat. Bake at 400° for 20 minutes or until tender and golden. Toss
with 1½ tablespoons melted butter and 1½ tablespoons chopped
fresh parsley. Combine ¼ cup reduced-fat mayonnaise, 2 teaspoons
fresh lemon juice, ⅛ teaspoon ground red pepper, and 1 minced
garlic clove. Serve with fries.

Vanilla low-fat ice cream with hot fudge sauce

257
calories

QUICK&EASY

Turkey and Cheese Panini

In Italian, panini means "small bread" and refers to a pressed sandwich. Using a grill pan gives the sandwich a nice appearance, but the recipe works just as well in a regular nonstick skillet. If you don't have provolone cheese, you can use mozzarella. Serve with tomato-bread salad.

2 tablespoons fat-free mayonnaise
4 teaspoons basil pesto
8 (1-ounce) thin slices sourdough bread
8 ounces sliced cooked turkey breast

2 ounces thinly sliced provolone cheese
8 ($\frac{1}{8}$-inch-thick) slices tomato
Cooking spray

1. Combine mayonnaise and pesto, stirring well. Spread 1 tablespoon mayonnaise mixture on each of 4 bread slices; top each slice with 2 ounces turkey, $\frac{1}{2}$ ounce cheese, and 2 tomato slices. Top with remaining bread slices.

2. Preheat grill pan or large nonstick skillet coated with cooking spray over medium heat. Add sandwiches to pan; top with another heavy skillet. Cook 3 minutes on each side or until golden brown. YIELD: 4 servings (serving size: 1 sandwich).

CALORIES 257; FAT 8.2g (sat 2.9g, mono 0.2g, poly 0.1g); PROTEIN 18.4g; CARB 30.4g; FIBER 4.1g; CHOL 30mg; IRON 2.4mg; SODIUM 1,208mg; CALC 204mg

QUICK TIP: You can find prepared pesto in jars, tubs, or tubes at most supermarkets.

SOUPS, SALADS, & SANDWICHES

Turkey and Cheese Panini

Tomato-bread salad
Combine 2 tablespoons each water and light mayonnaise, 1 table-spoon fresh lemon juice, and ¼ teaspoon hot sauce, stirring with a whisk. Combine 2 cups toasted French bread cubes, 4 cups halved cherry tomato, ½ cup each chopped fresh parsley and finely chopped red onion, ⅓ cup diced peeled avocado, and ½ teaspoon salt; toss with mayonnaise mixture.

Low-fat ice cream with sliced peaches

Nutritional Analysis

How to Use It and Why Glance at the end of any *Cooking Light* recipe, and you'll see how committed we are to helping you make the best of today's light cooking. With chefs, registered dietitians, home economists, and a computer system that analyzes every ingredient, *Cooking Light* gives you authoritative dietary detail like no other magazine. We go to such lengths so you can see how our recipes fit into your healthful eating plan. If you're trying to lose weight, the calorie and fat figures will probably help most. But if you're keeping a close eye on the sodium, cholesterol, and saturated fat in your diet, we provide those numbers, too. And because many women don't get enough iron or calcium, we can also help there, as well. Finally, there's a fiber analysis for those of us who don't get enough roughage.

Here's a helpful guide to put our nutritional analysis numbers into perspective. Remember, one size doesn't fit all, so take your lifestyle, age, and circumstances into consideration when determining your nutrition needs. For example, pregnant or breast-feeding women need more protein, calories, and calcium. And men older than 50 need 1,200mg of calcium daily, 200mg more than the amount recommended for younger men.

In Our Nutritional Analysis, We Use These Abbreviations

sat	saturated fat	**CHOL**	cholesterol
mono	monounsaturated fat	**CALC**	calcium
poly	polyunsaturated fat	**g**	gram
CARB	carbohydrates	**mg**	milligram

Daily Nutrition Guide

	Women Ages 25 to 50	Women over 50	Men over 24
Calories	2,000	2,000 or less	2,700
Protein	50g	50g or less	63g
Fat	65g or less	65g or less	88g or less
Saturated Fat	20g or less	20g or less	27g or less
Carbohydrates	304g	304g	410g
Fiber	25g to 35g	25g to 35g	25g to 35g
Cholesterol	300mg or less	300mg or less	300mg or less
Iron	18mg	8mg	8mg
Sodium	2,300mg or less	1,500mg or less	2,300mg or less
Calcium	1,000mg	1,200mg	1,000mg